FROM COLLEGE TO COVID TO RECESSION

A Guide to Making & Managing Money During an Economic Downfall

DISCLAIMERS

The information provided in this book is for informational purposes only and is not intended to be a source of advice or credit analysis with respect to the material presented. The information and/or documents contained in this book do not constitute legal or financial advice and should never be used without first consulting with a financial professional to determine what may be best for your individual needs.

The publisher and the author do not make any guarantee or other promise as to any results that may be obtained from using the content of this book. You should never make any investment decision without first consulting with your own financial advisor and conducting your own research and due diligence. To the maximum extent permitted by law, the publisher and the author disclaim any and all liability in the event any information, commentary, analysis, opinions, advice, and/or recommendations contained in this book prove to be inaccurate, incomplete or unreliable, or result in any investment or other losses.

Content contained or made available through this book is not intended to and does not constitute legal advice or investment advice, and no attorney-client relationship is formed. The publisher and the author are providing this book and its contents on an "as is" basis. Your use of the information in this book is at your own risk.

ACKNOWLEDGMENTS

First, let me thank God for guiding and watching over my life.

I would like to give a huge thank you to Stephney Riley, my mother/best friend/COO for not only giving me life but always speaking greatness over my life since birth.

Thank you to my dad, Erik Thomas, for always leading by example and for the life lessons I still carry to this day. Shoutout and much love to Triss, Mimi, and Janness.

Thank you to Nana, Papa, Aunt Donna, Aunt Erin, Uncle Cadell/Aunt Ginger, and the rest of the Thomas Family for putting that hustle and relentlessness in me.

Thank you to the Riley family for instilling love, care, and compassion in me.

Shoutout to all my friends that I consider family. I truly love y'all and appreciate the support. Special shoutout to Myles Moss; Blood couldn't make us any closer.

Shoutout to "Mr. Make a Play," a.k.a. Remy G. I couldn't ask for a better co-host of FYI FLI The Podcast, Chief Marketing Officer of FYI FLI, or friend.

Thank you to the economic and finance experts that provided their immense knowledge: Dr. Michael Thomas, Bernée E. Long, Arindam Nag, Jack Larimer, and Brandon of Worth Life Balance.

Thank you to Maryville College, especially Dr. Gallagher, Mr. Timmy, Twitch, Anne and Aimee, the Bonner Scholar Program, Coach Hayes, and Coach Cart.

Special thank you to my mentors, Johnny C. Taylor, Jr., and the rest of the FYI FLI advisory board: Luke Hohmann, Adam Sohn, Emilio Pineda, and Lisa Freberg.

A big thank you to my FYI FLI Team Day Ones: Lauren Long and Jennifer Colter. And this could not be possible without my editors, Martha Frase and Audrey Riley, and graphic designer, Sam Segal.

CONTENTS

CHAPTER 1: FROM COLLEGE TO COVID

This book really began in the fall of 2019. I was a college senior and student athlete at Maryville College in Tennessee who just started playing running back after switching from safety my first three years. It was just the fifth week of the season, and my head coach let me know that the game against our rivals Huntington was my chance to start if I did well in practice. There were four other running backs ahead of me, but none were producing as needed.

Keep in mind, I hadn't played running back since my sophomore year of high school in 2014. I had raw talent and ability, but what I lacked was patience. My coach worked on this with me, and by week two of the season, it clicked!

Honestly, I compared it to the EA Sports Madden Football game. On the newer Madden video games, you can't just hold the sprint button down the whole time. You have to be strategic when you accelerate and burst through an open hole, and that's what I did. I used my coach's tips and my Madden gameplay to fine-tune my running-back skills and boy did it start paying off. By the second week of the season, I began tearing the boys up in practice, breaking long run after long run. It was finally my time to shine.

I began week five going with the starters, just as my coach promised. I was confident and excited to finally get the shot I felt I deserved. And then...BOOM!

We did a simple running play in practice, not going too hard to preserve ourselves for Saturday's game against our rivals. The defense wrapped me up but didn't let me fall to the ground, and while I was standing, my teammate blocked another player to the ground. Unfortunately, there was something between my falling teammate and the ground. That something was my KNEE!

I immediately shouted something my mama would never want to hear me say and attempted to stretch it out. Knowing that this was my first opportunity to start at running back, I tried to push through and keep playing, but the pain was too much. I limped to the sideline and began stretching some more, and then I heard a very loud POP! At this point, I could put zero weight on my right leg. I hopped over to my coach and told him repeatedly, "I'm done... I'm done..."

I had torn my meniscus. My football season was over, forever.

This was a very tough and difficult situation to go through, considering this was my last year of playing college football. Looking back in my rearview mirror, that injury was a blessing in disguise. It propelled me to turn my energy and attention to writing my senior research paper.

I had chosen the topic of financial literacy for students and young adults because, looking around, I noticed the lack of financial education among my peers. I graduated with a major in business management and a minor in marketing, so I'd taken many classes dealing with money. I felt I had an above-average knowledge of the subject, but I worried about my peers in the arts, communications, criminal justice, and all the other majors that don't require any type of business or finance class? **If they weren't taught at home, then how could we expect our youth to graduate financially prepared for "adulting"?**

I realized just how much good information and insights I was collecting, and I thought it deserved a larger audience hungry for this kind of knowledge that just wasn't available in the K-12 or even college basic curriculum. I thought it would make a great book or guide for young people who want to take better control over their financial lives.

It was my cousin Myles who encouraged me to turn my research paper into a mobile app instead of a book.

Well, I'm the type of person that, when I hear a great idea, I'm going to turn that **idea** into **action**. So, from September to December 2019, I did nothing but research, research, research.

After having my knee surgery in December, I told my mom that when I got back to campus, I was going to meet with faculty and staff to share my idea until I worked my way up to the Dean of Students, and that's exactly what I did.

After hopping around on crutches to over 15 meetings, I secured my appointment for March 3, 2020, with Dean Klingensmith, my business professor Dr. Gallagher, and four other prominent faculty members. I presented the collection of financial literacy resources I hoped to turn into an app for young people.

This meeting went incredibly well, and there is one reason: **Preparation.**

I literally began preparing for the meeting three weeks prior, and for the first time in my life, I felt overprepared. Now there really is no such thing as being over prepared, but I want to emphasize how hard I worked to get ready and how much time I dedicated to that one moment. **Proper preparation truly does prevent poor performance!**

My fear of potentially blowing an amazing opportunity to present to the dean of Maryville College propelled me to ensure that I was 100% ready to knock it out of the park.

It was a relief to get that meeting over with, and as I waited for feedback. I turned my mind to one thought: my last Spring Break! Way back in November 2019, a group of 10 friends and I booked a 10-bed villa on the strip in Las Vegas. Everyone had already paid their share for the house and booked flights with no complications.

Then came March 13th; I will never forget that date. **That's the day the COVID-19 virus was officially acknowledged as a national threat**, and President Trump declared a state of National Emergency. In the days following, businesses, schools, and transport started shutting down. My friends and I anxiously watched the news and checked social media to see what was happening in Vegas.

Soon, all parties and events were canceled, then grocery stores and convenience stores emptied out with panic purchases. Finally, at 11:45 pm on March 15, Vegas announced it was shutting down casinos and going into full lockdown mode. That night, everyone was blowing up my phone, trying to see what we were going to do. Ultimately, my friends and I had to cancel the Airbnb and our flights, but that was the least of what we were about to face.

The next few days on campus were very strange. Tons of people had already left for spring break while my friends and I were still on campus. A lot of us were from out of state, thousands of miles from home. Eventually, the school made the decision that everyone should leave campus, and we would continue classes online.

It was a drastic change of plans for everyone. We thought we were going to be in Vegas turning up, but instead, we were all in shock about what was transpiring right in front of our eyes. The entire world was going on lockdown due to a global pandemic from some kind of virus called COVID-19.

I packed up as much stuff as I could and hopped on the road to Chattanooga, Tennessee, to take one of my friends home, and then to Atlanta to drop another friend off at the airport. Now alone, I reflected on the coming months as I drove the eight hours to my father's home in Florida, where I would finish off my senior year—virtually, on a computer screen.

Now let me tell you, this was one of the most challenging ordeals I have faced. You know what "senioritis" is, right? When a high school or college senior doesn't want to do anything but graduate! Well, imagine that times 200!

Not only was I ready to graduate, but now my mind, body, and spirit were in full entrepreneur mode as I worked toward building my financial literacy empire.

I began working for Delivery Dudes (Florida's version of DoorDash) to make some consistent income to put back into the business. That's all I was concerned about—making money and my new baby...I mean business!. I muddled through the last month of class and completed my four years in a grand celebratory fashion: Online Zoom Graduation.

My mom can literally tell you this story. She called me at the beginning of the ceremony and said, "Hassan, why didn't you tell me you were graduating today?"

My response? "I didn't know—I've been locked in." I was so focused on planting the seeds and building the foundation for my business that I missed my own graduation!

This determination was not unrewarded, though. In April 2020, around my birthday, I got a meeting with the President and CEO of the Society for Human Resource Management (SHRM) in the Washington, D.C., area. Johnny C. Taylor, Jr., a professional colleague of my mother, had recognized the immense potential of the financial literacy brand I was building and introduced me to the President of SHRM India, Achal Khanna, who connected me with her development team.

The developers and I got off to a great start. That is, until COVID went into full swing over there, and all communications between myself and the team in India ceased for a month and a half.

When they finally reached back out, I learned someone on their team had caught the virus. Now it was early August, and my website was supposed to be completed by the end of the month and the app a couple of months later. Nevertheless, **when God says no to one thing, he always says yes to another!**

I was determined to keep my momentum going on this new business I was launching. I called it **FYI FLI: For Your Information Financial Literacy & Investing.**

It wasn't my plan to target the traditional customers of financial advice— people with money to spend and invest. I wanted to help bridge the gap between education and entertainment for young Millennials and Gen Z who are struggling with small incomes, student debt, and poor credit, or who are perhaps trying to break out of generational poverty that may be plaguing their family and community.

I decided my next move was to start a financial literacy podcast.

Starting a podcast from scratch turned out to be no easy feat, but it is something I will never regret.

The most interesting part of creating the podcast was bringing all the material together for my audience of young Millennials and Gen Z. The process allowed me to interject myself into the financial literacy community and talk to influential and creditable entrepreneurs and educators in their respective fields.

I honestly believe that's what a podcast could do for you as well! Podcasting is a relatively new media, but it has already taken over streaming media, both audio and video. Business leaders and entrepreneurs understand that podcasts are the new way for people to digest information, and your podcast can be a vessel for information that a business wants to relay to its potential customers.

Every influencer, business owner, and even athlete should have a podcast. By getting out of your comfort zone and voicing your opinions, others will begin to trust you and value your expertise. Once you acquire that mantle of trust and credibility, you can monetize any and all offerings you can create.

Another reason starting a podcast was clutch for me and could do wonders for you is the **value exchange**. By definition, this is simply a transaction between two parties that results in each party receiving something of value or benefit from the transaction.

Value exchange is a key factor when speaking to your podcasts potential sponsors, guests, and business partners. You have to ask yourself, "How can I show how their involvement in this podcast benefits them as well as me"? **It has to be multi-benefical!**

This is how I was able to secure some of my most influential guests in our first season, including the actress and comedian GloZell; NFL player and owner of Sweet Ventures LLC William Sweet, and many other big-time business owners. They all have a story to tell—and a brand to promote—and I have a podcast where people will listen to an interesting and impactful story. Since August 2020, the FYI-FLI podcast has had over 35,000 downloads by listeners in 50-plus countries.

In 2021, I also began teaching financial literacy classes online and have conducted more than 50 so far, bringing this key information to individuals ranging in age from 5 to 60.

Our next step was securing our business foundation with a company called Centsai. Their support is allowing us to pair FYI FLI's diverse and relatable content with a certified national curriculum that we can take to high schools and colleges.

Our ambition is to implement our financial curriculum into every high school, college, and trade school in the world, because money is a global language that everyone wants to speak—fluently!

MY LOCKDOWN LESSONS

I want to share the five most important lessons I learned during the 2020-2021 COVID-19 pandemic.

1. Providing value is essential, but it's not number 1. Number 1 is to **keep faith in a higher power.**

As entrepreneurs, we often feel like we are self-made and that we are the ones making everything happen. But without God's grace, we are nothing. He is the one who chooses to bless us, but please don't think it's all just by faith.

James 2:14-26 says, "Faith without works is dead." Now, what does that mean? It means that simply believing in God is not enough; we must actively pursue his love and our dreams to be blessed in abundance.

Life is all about **balance** and **priorities**. During the pandemic, with churches and synagogues unable to have in-person services, some switched to virtual services. After some research to learn if any churches had podcasts, I found a couple that I really liked. One that stood out was "The Transformation Church" by Pastor Mike Todd and a couple of other incredible preachers.

This church's energy and relatable message made it a clear winner for me, but there are no losers—whoever is praising God and spreading the gospel has already won!

I am telling you this as an example of how you can add balance to your life. Even in lockdown, we don't have to sit around and listen to our favorite rappers or stream content all day. **We must balance our education, spiritual, and entertainment intake.**

It's okay to make small incremental changes. Nothing's wrong with listening to Drake and Roddy Rich 60% of the time, educational/self-improvement podcasts 20%, and spirit-based content 20%. You are balanced.

I came to realize that whatever you listen to or feed your spirit with, you actually begin to mimic. Let's make sure we're allowing a mixture of positive and enjoyable things into our spirit.

Keeping God first was a critical component for my success. For you, that may mean keeping some other form of belief in a higher power. When we are impacted by unforeseen life events like COVID, it helps a lot to have a spiritual force to believe in when it seems like the world is against us and nothing is right.

2. **Providing value** comes in at a strong number two. Whatever room you enter, you must do three things: **Show up, show out, and provide value!** That goes for bricks and mortar rooms as well as Zoom meeting rooms.

Those three things will assure you are remembered in a room alongside a bunch of big dogs and heavy hitters. We must be able to analyze everyone else's strengths and weaknesses, and once we do that, we must fill their weak cup from our strong cup.

I first realized I had a valuable offer while attending Earn Your Leisure's first InvestFest networking event in Atlanta. Most of the attendees were entrepreneurs, not podcasters. So, with that in mind, the smart move for me was to offer value to these entrepreneurs who did not already have a specified platform by providing them with just that—a place to tell their story and promote their brand at a time when podcasts were filling a huge void in people's locked-down lives.

Remember, value is something you exchange. So, now the entrepreneurs could provide me and my audience with valuable content based on real experiences from real people. Our audience would normally have to pay for this content in a coaching session, course, or expensive master class.

So, the moral of the story: **Lead with value, and all your relationships will be meaningful.**

But here's a warning—don't ever be naive and let people take advantage of you. When someone shows you their true actions and intent, believe them!

3. The third lesson is huge. **Eliminate all distractions and negativity**, including other people.

Let's just stop and think about how much time we have wasted on people who were not worth it. It's probably a lot. I'm glad you're reading this book, though, because, after this, they're going to think your name was K Camp the way you cut everyone off!

I'm kidding. You don't have to eliminate everyone who needs your time and attention, but those who are slowing you down from accomplishing your mission have to go. And you don't need to feel bad about it either!

We have only one life, and I know you're one of those people who puts everyone else before yourself. But your business is the child that you chose to bring into this world. Everything and everyone who isn't for the good of that child needs to be put aside.

At the same time you are taking care of your business, take care of yourself. You have to make sure **you are doing okay physically, mentally, and fiscally** before you can care for your business. At the end of the day, you are the one who has to deal with the rewards and consequences of every single choice you make, so why not make the choices that will yield the highest ROI for you?

After graduating and leaving college, I went through my Snapchat list, Instagram, and basically all my social media and unfollowed and distanced myself from people who never supported my company or me. These people were just taking up mental space and energy, especially because some of them were people I grew up with and who I expected to show nothing but love, as I always have.

This brings me back to my mom's advice, which is to **focus on your supporters and watch them grow!** This idea changed my life and allowed me to basically develop tunnel vision. I only give my time and energy to things that I have placed in my tunnel, like God, family, and FYI FLI. Other than them, I'm pretty much locked in.

4. The fourth lesson: **Live in reality.** This is a message for the ages because many of us choose to have a false sense of reality. Everything's okay, or it's not that bad. Just so we don't have to be the person to address the problem or come up with a solution.

Whether it be a false sense of reality about an addiction, health status, appearance, a significant other, or even business, we must do one of the hardest things: **Be honest with ourselves.** It is incredibly hard, and it's something you have to force yourself to do because of the results and the progression that will come from this self-honesty and awareness.

The first step in solving a problem is actually understanding the problem. So, If I can get you to believe in yourself enough to acknowledge and tackle the problems in your life, we have won.

Remember this: bad things happen. **But we must turn anger into action.** That's the only way to get over any negative thing that occurs in your life. Gotta make a plan and make a play! Simple as that.

For example, COVID-19 gave everyone in the world an unheard-of opportunity. We had the chance to be in our homes for over a year. The world that normally moves at a fast and relentless pace, slowed down and suddenly became still. This historical and unprecedented time could have been used in a multitude of ways.

Whether you used that time to self-pity or self-improve, this book will equip you with lessons and tips to increase productivity that will boost your confidence and execution skills. We will not harp on what you did or didn't do in the past. **What matters is your mindset and outlook on the future and how you plan on improving each day.**

5. Last major lesson learned during COVID: **Embrace fear, let go of self-doubt.**

After graduating from college to COVID, I jumped headfirst into starting a business. I did my first newspaper interview, my first radio interview, and taught my first webinar, all within the first two months of graduating college. Was I nervous? Heck yeah, I was! But what kept me from being unable to perform was my preparation.

As I mentioned before, it's true that proper preparation prevents poor performance. That preparation allows me to go into these classes I teach and different speaking engagements with confidence because I know I put the work into shine, and I deserve to succeed.

That's another thing—**you deserve it!** Please don't fall back on survivor's remorse—feelings of guilt because you were the one who made it out to strive toward your goals and success.

Yes, you and all your friends came from the same place, but did they put in the same amount of work as you? Did they make the same amount of sacrifices you had to make? God's blessings for you are for you and no one else. So please do not question the work you've put in.

Look fear in its face, accept it, and do it anyway! Accept and embrace the risk and do it anyway!

These lessons are what I've taken from a tough situation and turned into a blossoming business.

But now we are faced with another tough situation. A recession.

Full transparency: I was 10 years old during the 2008 recession, which happened to be one of the worst economic periods the U.S. has ever seen.

That's why I've sought out and collected expert analysis from the top economists and financial experts on what a recession is, how it will impact us, and how we can prepare to not only survive, but thrive during an economic downfall.

Workbook: Chapter 1: From College to COVID

1. Hassan gave 5 major lessons going 'From College To Covid': **Keep faith in a higher power, provide value, eliminate distractions, live in reality,** and **embrace fear**

   Which lesson can you relate to the most and why?

2. What has been your biggest lesson learned after going through COVID and quarantine?

3. Did you uncover any skills or passions? How can you turn that passion into profit?

CHAPTER 2: RECESSION

I'm not going to start this section off with the basic definition of a recession—that's coming. You really just want to know how being in an economic depression will affect your moola, your guap, your dinero— your money...But first, let's meet our recession experts.

Dr. Michael G. Thomas Jr., Ph.D., is an Accredited Financial Counselor (AFC®) and a lecturer at the University of Georgia. His research focuses on financial empathy, data visualization's effects on financial behavior, and the connection between brain function and money.

Utilizing financial empathy as a process for active listening and the creation of client-focused financial recommendations are reflected in two financial literacy and capability programs he helped co-create: Money Dawgs and Discovering Money Solutions.

Bernée E. Long, is a speaker, Gallup-Certified Strengths Coach, and the founder/owner and Chief People Officer of GENersection, a start-up talent identification, development, and placement company. GENersection specializes in guiding youth and young adults through the discovery and maximum utilization of their innate talents, focusing on intrapreneurship (business building), entrepreneurship, and leadership. GENersection's approach blends scientific research with practical life skills toward the goal of developing socially, professionally, and financially savvy adults who can make meaningful contributions to the workforce and society.

Brandon of Worth-Life Balance, a financial literacy coach that seeks to close wealth gaps by empowering people to build financial security. He is a proud husband and father, and despite humble beginnings has helped his family become first-generation multimillionaires.

Arindam Nag, an expert in financial education and how financial services firms can get involved in fostering financial literacy among its customers, in the workplace as well as in middle and high schools. Arindam understands the gap between Wall Street and main street, knowing how to break down often hard-to-understand financial topics for non-financial people. Founder of CentSai, the financial education platform that helps financial advisors, banks, credit unions and advisory platforms to embrace education, to improve public communication, and spread inclusion.

Jack Larimer, an experienced economist and research associate at Bridgewater Associates. Jack graduated from the University of Tennessee in 2019 and since then has used his experience in agriculture and petroleum pricing to catapult himself as one of the youngest economy researchers in his field.

WHO AND WHAT IS AFFECTED BY A RECESSION

You: The biggest threat to you personally is continued inflation, which makes everything more expensive and increases the potential for unemployment.

Small businesses: (Entrepreneurs) The biggest threat to your small business is continued inflation causing you to spend more money to get the products and supplies you need to run your business. This could have a multitude of negative effects on the financial health of your enterprise.

Big businesses: (Employees) Big businesses are in the same boat as small businesses. If you are reading this and you're an employee of a big business, then you may be at risk of layoffs caused by the increased cost to run the business as normal. But don't worry, we are going to touch on some of the things you can do to cover and prepare yourself.

Stock market: Share value typically goes down during a recession due to the loss of confidence in the economy, but for a savvy investor, a recession is like shopping on discount. Imagine going into a candy store and everything from the licorice to the fine chocolates are on sale! That's the scenario of the stock market during a recession.

People begin to feel afraid and pull their money out during an economic downturn. Many investors may want their cash liquid or easily accessible, but you have to consider that just like in life, the only time you lose is when you quit!

It's the same thought process in the stock market. The only time you lose money is when you sell your stock for less than you bought it for.

If you're reading this, I hope that you are a long-term investor like me, and if so, you know that over the last 100 years, the stock market has averaged a 10% return overall.

Since 1945, there have been 13 recessions and 25 bear markets—a.k.a. downward-trending markets.

Bull markets are markets trending upward. So, regardless of the market spiraling down, it will eventually come back up, because that's what markets do! As long-term investors, we don't care what's going on now, next year, or the year after that (depending on your time until retirement). We know and understand that over the long haul, if we keep investing in low-cost index funds and exchange-traded funds (ETFs) we will come out on top!

WHAT IS A RECESSION?

Before we continue, I want to make sure everyone is clear on what a recession is—from the technical definition and from the perspectives of the experts I've interviewed.

Economists say a recession is defined by **two consecutive negative quarters** (6 months) of declining Gross Domestic Product (GDP).

GDP is simply a calculation of all the goods, services, and products a country has produced quarterly or annually. **"GDP is the total production of a country,"** in the words of S&P economist Jack Larimer. So, whenever this number declines twice in a row, by definition you are now in an economic recession.

To dig deeper, Dr. Michael Thomas, professor of Finance at the University of Georgia, explains that there are four major expenditures that categorize GDP: **Consumer expenditure, business and investment expenditure, government expenditure,** and **net imports and exports.**

These are some of the categories that make up the overall GDP, but there are many different factors that can play a role, and that's why every recession is different.

This is why it can be very beneficial to stay up to date with world news, because a lot of the events that are happening globally have a cause-and-effect relationship with the prices we pay and the revenue we make from our businesses and investments.

Dr. Thomas provides this analogy: "All recessions aren't prolonged and cruel market collapses—some can be mild. I can have a cold and it could be mild, [but] that doesn't mean I didn't have a cold."

To relate that to a recession: Just because we aren't experiencing all three factors of **high unemployment, high inflation,** and **high interest rates** doesn't mean we aren't subject to one or two of those factors that we may need to be prepared for.

Workbook: Chapter 2: Recession

4. List some ways a recession could impact you? (pg.18)

5. True or False: You should pull all your money out of investments during a recession and save only cash (pg.18)

6. What is a simple way to define a recession? (pg.19)

7. What is Gross Domestic Product (GDP) (pg.19)

8. What are the four major expenditures that categorize GDP? (pg.19)

9. What are the three factors that makeup recessions? (pg.19)

HOW DO YOU PREPARE FOR A RECESSION?

I know you're expecting tips and tricks to prepare for an economic downturn, but I love the route that Dr. Thomas is taking. He says before we get into all of that, he wants us to **breathe and give ourselves some credit.**

You've already navigated through an unimaginable global pandemic; you've already dealt with and experienced inflated prices. So understand that you can and you will survive a recession. But the information learned in this book will help you thrive during this time.

Now the first tip: It **is critical to be aware of what you're spending and what you're making.** Your income and your expenses are the foundation for everything you do in personal finance.

When considering the rising prices of everyday necessities like gas, food, and housing, you will need to find a way to make more income to continue to increase the margin, or cushion, between your income and your expenses. Maintaining more income in relation to your expenses will give you the peace of mind of having disposable income. **This is the money you have left over after your mandatory expenses like rent, utilities, phone, insurance, etc., are met.**

Realistically, it comes down to having a plan. Bernée E. Long says, "The beauty of creating a plan is that you win when things go well and you win when things don't go well". This is all fact!

Let's say you are building a savings fund for a recession or an emergency. If that negative event never happens, and the danger is past, you have accumulated a pile of funds that you can tap for anything you want! Now if things do unfortunately go wrong, you're covered because you took the time to prepare for this.

Whenever you have a plan in a time of need it creates confidence and peace of mind while eliminating the feelings of stress and anxiety. Wouldn't you rather put in a little extra work to make sure that no matter what happens, you'll come out on top? That seems worth it to me.

Another gem Dr. Thomas touched on was finding a tribe or community you can relate to. You don't have to go around telling people how much you make or how much you have but find a couple folks that you can relate to in terms of your financial philosophy.

As humans, we're made to connect and congregate, and that's why COVID was so hard—everyone was isolated.

So, find a group or community that has the same goals as you. Whether that's a goal of building generational wealth, building our community up, or protecting and providing for our families, seek these people out because you never know where it can lead or the true impact it will have on your life.

Brandon of WorthLife Balance, a self-proclaimed "regular millionaire," states, "The worst time to do emergency planning is in the middle of an emergency!"

I interviewed five different experts in finance and economics, and they all agreed that an **emergency fund** was the number-one resource needed to prepare for a recession.

FYI FLI likes to call this a "peace of mind fund." Calling it a "rainy day" fund or emergency fund brings off negative vibes and we don't like that! Hearing the word "emergency" can make you automatically feel panicked, anxious, and worry-full.

A peace of mind fund is a set amount of money that you build for when—not **if** but **when**—something unexpected happens. This is so beneficial because having money to fall back on is literally what creates peace of mind!

In the past, experts usually recommended three to six months of your expenses saved up. Considering what we have been through with COVID-19 and the multi-year pandemic, we recommend at least six to twelve months saved up!

Pro tip: The best place to keep your peace of mind fund is in a **high-yield savings account (HYSA).** This account is literally the same as a regular savings account, but you get more bang for your buck!

You'll get paid more interest than a regular savings account because most of the time these high-yield accounts are online only.

This means that they can avoid the major expense of having an in-person location and are able to pass those savings along to you in the form of higher interest, which means more return on your money.

COMBATING POTENTIAL JOB LAYOFFS

One of the biggest factors that could impact us during a recession is a job layoff. This can be for a combination of reasons, but according to Arindam Nag, the two most significant reasons for layoffs are the increased cost to supply business products or the decreased rate of consumption from consumers, causing a lack of overall revenue.

Regardless of the reason, both could leave you jobless with no income, and we never want that to happen.

The most effective way to combat potential job loss is to invest. No, I'm talking about investing in stocks and crypto. I'm talking about making an investment in yourself! In order to become invaluable, we must first boost our skills and increase our knowledge in a relevant field.

Keyword: **relevant!** In your workplace, become a master at something only you or a few others can do. For example, everyone at your job can print papers, sign documents, and do manual, basic tasks. Not everyone can efficiently work and manipulate complicated software.

So, if you take the time to train and become certified in software that only a few others can use, who do you think your company will fire when employees have to be let go? The many people who can print and type or the few people who can print, type, and work the complicated software?

Increase your knowledge to increase your value. One of my favorite sayings on the podcast is, "The more you learn—the more you earn."

We're young, so sometimes we may feel we know everything. Many of us, including myself, usually try to rely on our own strengths and knowledge. While it is great to believe in yourself, the saying, "You don't know what you don't know" is indeed a true statement.

Bernée E. Long, speaker, trainer, and founder of GENersection, an intergenerational talent development company, is an advocate of identifying your own unique and innate talents, developing them into strengths, and learning how to leverage them.

She encourages young people to double down on their top strengths while managing their "lesser strengths" by surrounding themselves with those who have strengths in their weaker areas. "Never underestimate the power of TEAM," she says.

Bernée believes that learning is a two-way street and we can learn from each other regardless of generational divides. Stressing the importance of lifelong learning as essential to adding value, she credits her regular interactions with young people with helping her from "becoming obsolete" and continuing to add value to the world.

I asked Bernée what would be the most important lesson she's learned about acquiring skills and strengths to become more valuable. She said: "Constantly challenging my thinking and mindset is not only the most important lesson that I have learned, but it is also the toughest work that I have done and will continue to do for the rest of my life.

"I believe the best leaders and humans are those who are willing to do the hard work of regularly looking in the mirror. They may not always like how they show up, but they are willing to continuously course-correct," said Bernée.

Another major factor that can help you survive a layoff, according to Jack Larimer, is to be knowledgeable about your job and its specific sector. Do people need your goods or services? Is it essential to their survival?

If so, Larimer says you're probably in a safe spot, because regardless of the economic downfall, you will still be in demand.

On the other hand, if you find yourself in a risky, non-critical position in a recession, then you must take it upon yourself to find ways to bring in extra streams of income—whether that be a side hustle, a second job, or your own business. We will go into many types of side hustles and ways you can bring more income in our "Making Money" section of the book

WHAT IS INFLATION AND WHAT CAUSES IT?

"Inflation is not always bad," says Arindam Nag, CEO of Centsai Financial Education. "You want inflation, because that means your economy is growing, but if your economy isn't growing faster than inflation, that's where the issue lies."

Inflation is the increased cost of goods and services, but what actually causes inflation?

Dr. Thomas encourages us to think about it logically. Over the last couple years, with COVID-19 and quarantine, people are more eager to get out of the house and spend like never before.

On the other hand, as we've discussed, the supply chain issues and increased cost to produce goods and services mean businesses have not been able to meet the overwhelming demand.

Remember high school economics? As demand runs high with a low supply, prices will hit the sky. (You see that rhyme I did there?) But in all seriousness, this is what causes inflation to rise—the imbalance of supply and demand.

Normally, you would think that when prices are higher, people will slow down on spending. But again, we are in unprecedented times due to increased consumer spending after a multi-year pandemic.

This increased spending is another factor that entices the Federal Reserve to raise interest rates. **Their goal is to make it more expensive for you to borrow money, while incentivizing you to save money.**

You may ask though, why in the world would the government not want us to spend money? Dr. Thomas explains that if the government can slow down consumer spending for a bit, supply chains and production have time to rev back up. This will provide the proper balance of supply and demand and should hopefully bring prices back down.

It's basically a huge balancing act that the government and federal reserve are doing—. raising interest rates to lower inflation and slow spending. But when spending becomes too slow. then rates need to be lowered to encourage consumer spending.

I'm glad this is not my job, but learning what is going on in our macro and micro economy will pay huge dividends as you can now be more prepared and ahead of financial downturns and changes in the market.

Workbook: Chapter 2: Recession

10. What is the money called that you make from a job, side hustle, or business? (pg.21)

    A. Profit

    B. Revenue

    C. Income

    D. Expense

11. What is the money called that you spend? (pg.21)

    A. Dividend

    B. Expense

    C. Income

    D. Gone

12. What is the money called that's available to spend after mandatory expenses are paid? (pg.21)

13. Why is it good to have a plan? (pg.21)

14. True or False: The worst time to do emergency planning is in the middle of an emergency. (pg.22)

15. What is a "peace of mind" fund"? (pg.22)

16. Where is the best place to keep your "Peace of Mind Fund"?(pg.22)

17. Why does job loss impact us during a recession? (pg.23)

18. The most effective way to combat job loss is by investing in: (pg.23)

    A. Stocks

    B. Real Estate

    C. Yourself

    D. Crypto

19. The more you LEARN - the more you EARN? True or False (pg.23)

20. What is inflation? (pg.25)

21. In this particular recession, why does the government want us to refrain from spending money at a fast rate? (pg.25)

HOW MICRO AND MACROECONOMICS IMPACT OUR LIVES

It can be very difficult to stay aware of macroeconomics when your microeconomics are in turmoil.

Macro is what's going on in the world on a grand scale. **Micro** is what's going on in your immediate neighborhood, city, or state.

For example, a major reason cars and electronics have reached some of the highest prices ever is due to semiconductors or the lack of them (macro). Taiwan is the largest producer of semiconductors, and with tensions rising between the U.S. and China, it will likely become even more difficult to import these semiconductors.

Although the US has been pushing heavily to bring semiconductor plants to major tech cities like Austin and Seattle, it's still hard to compete with the low cost of labor and production overseas.

Now you may ask, "Okay Hassan, nice to know, but how does this impact me?" This macroeconomic occurrence impacts you because almost everything you and I use is powered by semiconductors—our computers, cars, phones, TVs, appliances, video games, and even medical technology.

So if it becomes more expensive for a business to acquire a semiconductor, it will also become more expensive to buy items that use semiconductors.

This is only one example of how macroeconomics impacts our everyday lives. Another practical example would be the war in Ukraine affecting our gas prices. Russia is one of the world's biggest oil suppliers. So, when President Biden banned Russian imports, it caused a huge spike in prices in December of 2021.

So this just goes to show that these two events—Russia's war on Ukraine and President Biden's reaction has caused gas prices to go up, directly impacting our pockets!

WHAT HAPPENS WHEN THE FEDERAL RESERVE INCREASES INTEREST RATES?

Basically, this causes an increase in what it costs to borrow money. Any loan you may want to take out, like a mortgage, car loan, or credit card, will be costlier than before. But at the same time, the amount of interest you will receive for saving money increases.

According to Brandon of Worth Life Balance, that is the purpose of raising interest rates: to decrease spending and increase savings rates to balance the economy out.

Be sure to take advantage of these high interest rates by saving your cash in HYSAs, which usually give a higher rate of return on your money than traditional savings accounts.

The problem the Federal Reserve—the "Fed"— faces whenever it tries to stabilize inflation by raising interest rates is that this move can end up stopping growth of our economy.

Consequently, if we don't slow down spending, we will spend ourselves into a recession. So the Fed is forced into a big juggling act between raising and lowering interest rates to keep the economy growing at a steady rate to avoid a major recession.

HOW INTEREST RATES CAN WORK FOR YOU OR AGAINST YOU

As we mentioned above, the definition of **interest** is the cost to borrow or lend money. Whenever you save money or invest in something that pays interest, you are basically being incentivized to keep your money in the bank or the investment. So as interest rates rise, so does the amount you're getting back on the money you saved and invested.

This is when Jack Larimer tells us to watch and be careful not to fall victim to the contrary. Whenever interest rates rise, they do help people who are saving and investing, but they also significantly cripple and punish people who are **borrowing and in heavy debt!**

For example, if someone had credit card debt during the period of recession, then unfortunately it will cost them more to continuously borrow and use the bank's money due to high interest rates.

This applies to car loans, mortgage loans, or any type of loan or borrowing that you're considering. So be aware of any and all debts you may incur during this period of uncertainty.

All in all, the two fundamental facts about recessions is that **they are normal** and **none are exactly the same.**

Workbook: Chapter 2: Recession

22. What is macroeconomics? (pg.30)

23. What is microeconomics? (pg.30)

24. Why is it important to be knowledgeable about what's going on in the world? (pg.30)

25. What happens when The Federal Reserve "The Fed" increases interest rates? (pg.31)

26. What is the purpose of raising interest rates? (pg.31)

27. What happens if The Federal Reserve increases interest rates too much? (pg.31)

28. What does interest mean? (pg.32)

29. When interest rates rise they help people that are saving and investing - they also significantly cripple and punish people who are borrowing and in heavy debt! True or False (pg.32)

A SHORT HISTORY OF U.S. RECESSIONS

According to Bloomberg.com, since 1945, the U.S. has seen 13 recessions and 25 bear markets. Recessions on average usually come every six to eight years, but before 2020, the country set a record by going a decade without a recession.

Some of the worst recessions have led to economic factors like productivity decreases in industry, decreases in consumer spending, and increases in unemployment and inflation.

This recession we are technically in has many contributing factors. Effects of the pandemic, Russia's **war** on Ukraine, political turmoil, and high levels of consumer spending. But as I mentioned, recessions are a normal part of the rhythm of an economy and have happened throughout U.S. history. Here's some background on the recessions that have impacted the U.S.

Longest Recession: The Great Depression (1929-1939)

Although every recession is different, The Great Depression is known as one of the worst economic downturns in American history. It lasted 10 long years as was caused by multiple factors: inflated economic projections, agriculture and industrial production setbacks, and the stock market crash of 1929.

Before the crash, the economy was booming. Society labeled this era "the roaring 20s," but as 1930 approached, things began to wobble. A historic major drought slowed the production of food and agriculture as fields turned to dust and people were forced off their land. Unemployment started to rise, but so did the stock market.

But wait a minute. If companies were losing money and cutting employees, how were their stock prices still rising?

Can you start to see the mechanisms here? Whenever the U.S. is over-leveraged or makes inflated projections, it usually leads to a negative backlash when those projections don't come to fruition. So, inflated projections lead to a stock market plummet, causing shareholders to start panic-selling their stocks and businesses to lose money.

Employees are laid off, creating a growing jobless population and a multitude of other negative effects that fall like dominos. It's said that at one point nearly 15 million Americans were unemployed, and almost half of U.S. banks failed.

<u>Worst Financial Crisis in U.S. History: 2008-2009 Recession</u>

Another huge recession that impacted millions of people came in 2008. That's the one I lived through but barely remember. To break down the factors of this recession, we need only look at the late 2000s' landscape of predatory lenders, the overvalued housing market, and consumers being over leveraged with debt.

The first mistake that led to this recession were the loose rules and regulations governing private mortgage lenders. These lenders offered tricky and sometimes even fraudulent loans to new homebuyers and current homeowners looking to refinance.

Many consumers thought they were getting great deals on property due to incredibly low interest rates and few restrictions **on borrowers. This brought people with otherwise poor financial prospects into the real estate market and encouraged even experienced** investors **to over-extend themselves. When** the economy started to react and forced house prices to fall below their mortgaged value, millions of borrowers could not pay their mortgages, losing their homes and causing banks to be left with properties they couldn't sell.

<u>Most Comparable to Today: 1982-1983 Recession</u>

Jack Larimer believes the 1982 recession is the most similar to what we are going through today. Granted, we aren't seeing inflation of 14% like the early 1980s, but the similarities are certainly there. Jack says it is comparable because it was caused by an extreme interest rate hike by then-Fed Chair Paul A. Volcker in order to control hyperinflation during that time. If we fall deeper into a recession this year, it is likely to be caused by the raising of interest rates to lower inflation, which in turn could slow U.S. growth.

The 1982 recession is known as the "double dip" recession," as the U.S. experienced an earlier recession in 1980—another comparable situation. Although we weren't in a recession in 2020 and 2021, we experienced many of its characteristics because of the pandemic, like (temporary) high unemployment rates, rising costs, and a decrease in production. Now in 2023, we have officially experienced a recession by the technical terms of two continuous quarters of declining GDP.

I believe this is where history becomes interesting and impactful. We know from our predecessors in the 1980s that raising interest rates absurdly high will bring down inflation but will also stunt our growth.

So this is the balancing act the Fed has to perform. Sounds like a tough position to be in, but realistically we can't control what they do.

My football coach always said, "Control the controllables." Meaning, focus your time and energy only on the things you have the ability to control.

<u>Are We Consumers Causing This Recession?</u>

This is something I hadn't heard of before—a "consumer-led recession." Jack says the purpose of the Fed raising interest rates is to make goods and services cost more, which will make people spend less. (It hasn't so far.) Jack gave a great analogy describing who is at fault here—the Fed or the consumer (us). He says putting the blame on either side is the same as asking who is responsible for a touchdown: the quarterback or receiver? Both parties are contributors!

To give a realistic example: We know that everyone wanted to travel more after lockdown, so the demand for gas has increased. As we know, when demand goes up, supply goes down, increasing prices. And, Russia invaded Ukraine, also causing gas prices to go up.

Clearly, there are a multitude of factors causing changes in our economy, but putting the blame or fault on one side isn't logical, because we are dependent on and reactive to what happens in our world. To be honest, no one truly knows 100% what is going to happen next!

When thinking about a recession, there are a few main factors that impact our finances and our lives. Unemployment would normally be the biggest factor, but this recession we are in right now does not follow that suit. This is due to a ton of different factors stemming from historically low unemployment rates, COVID, and gig and remote work. Still, necessities like food, gas, and housing are now much more expensive. So, the money that would have been saved or invested now has to be put into everyday needs that just last year did not cost as much!

Political Propaganda and Recession Fear-mongering

In times of economic and social change, it is very important to be thoughtful about what you're hearing and not fall victim to dramatic headlines. Money, as we all know, is a huge psychological and emotional factor for everyone. So, when money and markets are affected, many politicians will use any negative news to blame and frame the opposing side.

When you have influential political figures using words like "depression" and "recession," it can spark an emotional reaction in many people. This can cause people to start changing their habits, like saving more and spending less. Media-driven emotional reactions can also cause people to overreact—like buying up all the water and toilet paper. I know you all remember that!

Our advice: Do your own research and make the best decisions for you and your family instead of seeing one eye-catching headline and running with it!

Beware of fear-mongering—**the act of creating a narrative that incites fear in people.** Companies will try to do this because fear and uncertainty creates dependence, and if you come to depend on a company, they will have you as a lifelong customer!

So, you have to analyze and check different sources to see if the information you're receiving is consistent. Use the company's information as a tool to make decisions; don't let them end up using you as a tool to increase their profits. Dr. Thomas says we must **"audit our systems." Keep tabs on** information and sources you are allowing into your life that may create trauma or anxiety for you.

How Much Money to Save During a Recession?

Everyone talks about saving money, especially during a time of economic turmoil. CEO of Centsai Financial Education Arindam Nag says, "A good rule of thumb is to save at least one-third of your income." Now in all fairness, he said his own father gave him this advice, but Arindam has adjusted it for the times we live in today. "At the minimum, we should be saving at least 15% of our income."

Why should we save in the first place? The reason is to create peace of mind that comes with knowing that when (not if) an emergency happens, we're good because we have funds to fall back on. That is what creates peace of mind.

We should be saving at least 6 to 12 months of our expenses. Everything after that should be invested!

We'll talk more about this in our **Managing Money** section of the book, but something to highlight now is the importance of simply knowing what is coming in and what is going out. **The basic rule of personal finance is to understand your income vs. your expenses**.

Here is step-by-step breakdown for creating your own budget that will enable you to understand the basics of your financial situation:

- Make three tabs in Excel or Google Sheets

- Label them for the previous three months (for example, June, July, August)

- For each month, calculate your total income from all sources (your job, side hustle, allowance, child support, rental income, etc.

- Review your bank statements over the past three months and list all expenses for each month, assigning every expense to a general category. This helps you know and understand all your spending categories (housing, utilities, car note, eating out, subscriptions, etc.).

To find out how much you spend on average in each category, total the amount from each category for each month and divide by three to find your average expenditure, which will dictate your budget for that category. If you spent $90 on food in June, $150 in July, and $115 in August, your monthly target for spending on food is $118. If you want to cut expenses, aim for a lower target—say, $100.

To figure out your total expenses and income, add together all the income and expense categories for each month, total them, and divide both amounts by three. Subtract your total expenses from total income and everything left is your **disposable income** that can be used however you please.

Example: $3000 Income - $1500 Expenses = $1500 Disposable Income.

Remember to take into account your pay frequency if you're on a fixed annual salary. It's simpler to set a monthly budget if you are paid monthly (12 paychecks) or bi-monthly (24 paychecks), because you have the same amount of money coming in every month. But if you are paid every two weeks, you will receive 26 paychecks each year. Two months during the year you'll get three paydays! To figure out your monthly income in this case, multiply your paycheck by 26, then divide by 12.

To stay on track and out of the negative at the end of the month, your expenses, including what you put aside monthly for savings, should come in below that number.

Show Yourself the Love

Looking forward, keep in mind that recessions will come and they will go. The U.S. is a market, and just like any market there will be ups and downs. But with the knowledge you're taking from this book, you will have the tools and confidence to not only survive, but thrive into the future.

I believe we should all be striving for financial freedom and financial wellness. But what does that look like? Dr. Thomas describes financial wellness as the ability to **"live for today and plan for tomorrow."** This quote is so impactful because often we feel like money management and budgeting is closely associated with sacrifice and restriction.

This is not the case. Budgeting and investing can be viewed as showing your future self some love, not a momentary sacrifice. Becoming financially literate or educated in money management gives you the ability to not only live for today, but plan for tomorrow as well!

If we were to ask people of retirement age (65+) what their biggest regret is, 9 out of 10 would say, "I wished I saved more money when I was younger". We cannot blame them, because there weren't nearly as many resources, tools, and technologies readily accessible back then, especially for minority communities.

Nowadays, we have no excuse. The abundance of accessible information has brought financial freedom within arms' reach for all of us.

If you feel trapped in your physical environment, then start changing your virtual environment.

What I mean by that is: Begin to balance your entertainment with content that is more educational and life-building. What you consume and listen to on the daily is a major factor in the confidence and belief you have in yourself. Without that confidence, belief, and knowledge, it will be very hard to build generational wealth.

Good thing you have chosen to read this book, because this next section will show you not only how to make money but manage it as well. This knowledge will lead to the confidence and belief that you can and you will become financially free for you and your family!

Workbook: Chapter 2: Recession

30. Which recession lasted the longest? (pg.34)

31. Which recession is known as the worst ever? (pg.35)

32. Which recession is closely associated with our current recession? (pg.35)

33. Due to the recession our everyday items like food, gas, and housing cost the same as the year before? True or False (pg.35)

34. What is fear-mongering? (pg.36)

35. According to the CEO of Centsai Financial Education, Arindam Nag, how much should we save? (pg.37)

36. Why should we save money? (pg.37)

CHAPTER 3: HOW TO MAKE MONEY DURING AN ECONOMIC DOWNFALL

Want to make money while in high school or college? Would you like to travel the world without worry? How about never having to work for another controlling boss? How would it feel to be able to help your loved ones in their time of need?

All these options can become reality when you have financial freedom.

Financial freedom is having the time and options to do whatever you want, whenever you want. When we don't have money or the knowledge to make it grow, our time and our decisions are out of our control.

Lack of money will have us trading all our time for green pieces of paper. Before we make any decision, we have to check our bank accounts to see if money will allow us to buy that certain item or book that trip we've always wanted to go on.

That's why we have to master our money or it will become the master of us.

The first step to mastering your money is to **make more of it!** Other financial gurus will tell you to cut back on your expenses and spend less. Yes, that's a good option, but there is only so much you can cut back. Everyone has mandatory and basic necessities that cost money, like food, utilities, transportation, and housing.

On the other hand, making more money comes with no maximum or minimum. Breaking it down in the simplest terms possible: **We have to increase the margin—or the difference—between how much money we make and how much money we spend.**

This is the true key to managing your money. For example, if you're making $10,000 and spending $9,999 on things that aren't producing more income, then you're hustling backwards.

The goal is to make as much money as possible while maintaining or decreasing the amount we spend so we can invest and save the difference. As mentioned above, there are only so many expenses that can be cut down or lowered. So, that's where making more money comes in. This is the way to increase the margin between our income and expenses.

Why is this so important? This margin is what allows you to have discretionary income—a.k.a. spendable income. This is the money that can be spent on literally whatever you want **but is available only** after we have our bills, investments, savings, and mandatory expenses covered.

Now, I'm sure you're asking yourself, "How can I make extra money when I'm already working a 9 to 5?" In this day and age, we are blessed to have access to an abundance of resources and opportunities thanks to the internet. So, in this section, we'll uncover eight ways to make money online in the comfort of your own residence. Let's get into it!

EIGHT ONLINE SIDE HUSTLES

Earning money online has never been as easy as it is now. All it requires is a computer, a smartphone, and a solid internet connection.

Most of these opportunities do not need special skills or qualifications before getting started, but they do require an understanding of how to complete the task and solve a need or problem.

As the digitization of our world progresses, legitimate opportunities to make money online are rapidly expanding, and millions of people do it each day. But we are going to focus on eight different approaches.

- Dropshipping
- Starting a unique blog
- Market research
- Reselling ebooks
- Transcription and translation
- Creating a course
- Tutoring
- Data entry

Picture all the excess cash that will be at your disposal with your 9 to 5 income plus your newly found online side hustle! With all that extra currency, it can be tempting to spend frivolously, but it's truly not about how much you make. It's about how much we can **keep, save, and invest.**

So, after we discuss the eight best ways to make money, we will then touch on proper money management practices and smart investing strategies. So let's dive in!

Dropshipping

Dropshipping is an order fulfillment option that allows e-commerce businesses to outsource procuring, storing, and shipping products to a third party, typically a supplier. The dropshipping model commonly appeals to entrepreneurs seeking efficiency and low overhead, but it can come at a cost.

To break it down in the simplest terms possible, there are three parties involved: **the customer, the dropshipper (you), and the third-party supplier.**

When a customer orders a product from a retail website, normally the seller will process the order and locate the inventory (physically stored in a warehouse or storage facility), then ship out the physical product and collect payment.

The major benefit of dropshipping is that it removes the labor of **acquiring and storing** inventory and shipping, freeing the seller to focus on marketing and customer service.

Simply, the customer orders the product from your website, you notify the third-party supplier, and they package up and deliver the ordered products. So where does your profit come in?

When dropshipping of any kind, the seller will add a **profit margin** to your product. The supplier gives you their total price, and you add what you'd like to make as a profit to that. Keep in mind that e-commerce is very competitive, so profit margins need to be realistic.

Setting product prices can be a trial-and-error process. You'll quickly learn from experience what your customers are willing to pay for the products offered. Most people with a dropshipping business set around 20% to 30% profit margins.

Here's what that transaction looks like:

- The third-party supplier is charging $10 for a toy.

- You advertise that toy on your website, marking it up to $20.

- A customer buys your $20 toy for their child.

- You purchase the $10 toy while giving the third-party supplier your customer's shipping information.

- The third-party supplier ships the toy to the customer.

- You take your $10 profit, and everyone's happy.

You need to consider the items you're selling, too. A lower-priced item might be more popular and provide a regular income, but a higher-priced item will mean greater profit margins.

Dropshipping is such a good move because you don't have to pay for shipping or store inventory. You only order the items your customer has already paid for, then sit back and collect your profit.

As with any store, whether it be brick-and-mortar or online, you will need to focus strongly on marketing and customer service to truly grow.

Here are five simple steps to start making money with dropshipping:

Set up your website hosting. There are many options you can choose from here, but some research is needed. Some of the best startup sites to check out are Bluehost.com, Ionos.com, Hostgator.com, Shopify.com, and Wordpress.com.

This is where some of your upfront costs will occur. Once connected, you can then customize your site for the aesthetic you want, and even add apps to enhance customer experience. These apps and plugins will help make your e-commerce store as efficient and attractive as possible, which is the best way to increase sales and scale growth.

Decide on your niche. What products do you want to sell? Who do you want your customer to be? Think about the audience size and profit potential of your products. Some will appeal to a broad range of people, such as household items, but you'll also have more competition if your products are everyday essentials.

Don't let the competition stop you though. When you go into the grocery store, how many different name-brand loaves of bread do you see? Over 20! Find what makes you unique and a bit different from the rest, and go gain market share!

Although a highly competitive market shouldn't flat out scare you into another area, being in a niche market, even with its smaller audience, will be less competitive for marketing. You'll also likely have more success with high-priced items if your store is very niche.

For example, food products have a very broad market, but if you were to only sell vegan items, that would be an example of niching down. Yes, your customer base is smaller, but so is your competition, so with great marketing you have a higher chance of standing out.

Find your dropship suppliers. You'll need to find third-party suppliers of the products you want to sell who will be reliable and trustworthy. Some of the best advice I've received from dropshippers is to use recommendations and referrals. If someone you know has had good experiences with a supplier, then that could be a good option for you as well.

Use social media, Facebook groups, hashtags, etc. to find a community of drop shippers so you are not going into this new world alone. You could do this manually, or you can use free apps like Modalyst, AliExpress, and so on. This will save you lots of time when it comes to finding the best dropshipping products for your store.

Design your storefront. Depending on the amount of time and experience you have, you can either do this yourself by utilizing the tons of free online tutorials, or hire a front-end web designer. It all depends on how confident you are with digital technology.

The best part about doing it yourself is that you can teach yourself as you go along. I like to call it **building the plane while flying**!

That'll reduce your ongoing website development costs. You can also add products and change the website design as your business grows without having to contact someone externally. Finding ways to become self-sufficient and automate your processes will put you on a fast track to success.

Keep in mind the buying experience should be as easy as possible for your customers. This means supplying clear and attractive product pictures alongside relevant information. The easier it is for customers to find and view products on the site, the more likely you will sell them. In this day and age, it's all about customer convenience!

Develop a marketing strategy. Once your website is set up, it's time to start marketing your ecommerce business.

Social media is the best and fastest way to increase sales for dropshipping websites. Plan to promote your business or individual products on the platform your target customers use the most.

Some products are best advertised on Facebook. Others, like home and interior design products, may perform better on Pinterest. Investigate your target audience to see which social media platforms they use most.

Gen-Z likes to spend their time on TikTok and Instagram, while Millennials seem to prefer Instagram and Twitter. And every generation before is most likely on Facebook.

You can post on all social media sites to see which one gets the most traction. From there, whichever works the best, double down your efforts, run some paid ads, and continue to scale your business!

You can also create a group or community by launching an e-commerce newsletter. Set up a form on your website enabling people to sign up to receive emails from you. This allows you to easily promote a particular product each week to increase sales.

<u>Start a Unique Blog</u>

Blogging is one of the oldest ways to make money online, and if you like to write, it's still a great way to earn on a part-time or full-time level. Many people start blogging with a niche focus. Topics should be narrow enough to build loyal followers—like a particular model of car, a money making idea like dropshipping, or overcoming a habit like procrastination—and broad enough to inspire a lot of unique and engaging content.

One of the most important keys to creating a blog is to **establish a community**. The best approach is to have an overarching theme or purpose to your blog. Meaning, find a problem, issue, or interest that people care about and attach your mission to aspects of this theme your audience can relate to in their everyday lives.

When people are able to relate to and interact with what you're writing about, they begin to feel they are a part of something bigger than just you or them. That is how you build a community.

You can feature your blog on a variety of platforms. Shopify and WordPress are great places to begin. When you start blogging, focus on very specific keywords. As you grow, continue to expand and see which topics do the best with your audience.

Once you've analyzed the data on what's working, double down and give your audience what they want. This is how to start building a following of readers who actually care about you and your content.

There are several ways to promote and eventually make money on your blog:

- Include affiliate links from other companies in your posts.

- **S**trategically place ads in your posts.

- Sponsored posts can help you monetize a particular brand that pays you. This is popular with review bloggers who talk about products they actually use.

- Sell digital or physical products on your blog page.

- Use your blog to build a personal brand that helps you earn speaking engagements and paid appearances, and could even blossom into a podcast or book. Or maybe both!

Here are a few typical blog topics to find a niche within and start making money as a blogger:

- Fashion
- Food
- Sports
- Travel
- Lifestyle
- Parenting
- Gaming
- Do-It-Yourself

Follow these five simple steps to start your blog:

1. Choose your blog name and set up your hosting. When choosing a name, be sure to pick something creative, but not anything too crazy or off the wall in that people won't know what your blog is about. In this day and age, everyone's attention span is so short.

If your blog name doesn't immediately catch people's attention and doesn't resonate with what you're talking about, then it will be tough to draw people to your blog.

Choose a catchy and creative name that lets people know right away the topic or theme of your blog. If it's good enough, your reader will be hooked, and all you have to do is bring them the content to make them a lifelong fan.

To publish your blog, you will need to have a **blogging platform** and a **hosting platform.**

The blogging platform is where you will create, edit, and format your blog. The hosting platform is where your blog's files, data, and information will be stored so it is never lost. Without a hosting site, your blog will not be readily accessible by the public.

2. **Pick a simple design theme** to make your blog your own. Your design should be relative not only to your topic, but to your audience as well. If you are creating a blog about peace and meditation, avoid bright flashing animation or any design elements that detract from your calming content. Craft your look and feel to the message you want your audience to receive.

3. **Add blogging plugins** to find your readers and track stats via WordPress. Plugins are basically upgrades to your blog site. These tools can drive engagement by offering a more convenient checkout, automatic emails to people who leave your blog, etc. These plugins are there to improve the quality and function of your website.

4. **Write compelling content** to create a blog that your readers love. Give your readers something to care about and look forward to!

5. **Promote your blog.** Growth is virtually impossible without a proper marketing and advertising strategy. You put time and effort into your work. Be proud of what you've created! Employ marketing strategies to get your work in front of others.

Market Research

The key to any successful business is knowing what your customer wants and delivering it. One of the best lessons I learned going from college to COVID is that it doesn't matter what I want. It matters what the customers want and need.

When I'm making a podcast or preparing to speak, I'm not thinking about what I want to say. I'm thinking about what my audience wants to hear and what will impact them the most! It's hard to craft a message or a product without knowing what the customer needs. At the end of the day, business is all about solving a customer's needs so well they will pay you for it—trading money for the value you provide.

Market research is the action of gathering information about consumers' needs and preferences. Businesses often use this form of market research when they have a smaller budget or when ample market research has already been performed on a particular topic. An example of market research is conducting an online search and making note of the most recent data published on that particular topic.

There are two main types of paid market research: **surveys** and **focus groups.**

Market survey research involves analyzing a given market to gain insight into the buying potential and attributes of the target audience for a product or service. It assures the success of a new concept or established product, as it focuses on collecting feedback from a target audience to understand their demographics, expectations, and needs.

You can make money filling out these surveys through companies like Survey Junkie, which helps their clients develop products and services for their audience., It's also a very good example of a side hustle that is fun, flexible, and free to you. Survey Junkie's average pay is slightly above the industry standard at $0.20 to $3.50 per survey. In terms of an hourly rate, you may earn between $2 and $5 per hour.

The fact that Survey Junkie is a free platform that lets users answer questions in exchange for PayPal cash or gift cards makes it one of the best side hustles to make money online.

Focus groups are designed to provide exploratory rather than conclusive research data so marketers can understand not only what their customers think, but also how and why they think the way they do. The main goal and objective of a market survey is to collect data surrounding a target market such as competitor analysis, pricing trends, and customer expectations.

Participating in a focus group generally pays more than surveys, with the top-earning groups offering from $50 to $100 for your time. You'll probably be given free samples of products as well.

Workbook: Chapter 3: Making Money Online

37. Drop shipping is a good business model because you can avoid paying for shipping and store inventory. True or False (pg.43)

38. What are the three parties involved with drop shipping? (pg.43)

    A. The customer, The drop shipper (you), and The third-party supplier.

    B. The consumer, The director, and The fulfiller

    C. The creator, The distributor, and The fiddler

    D. The customer, The dump taker, and The third-party supplier.

39. One of the biggest keys to creating a blog is to establish a: (pg.47)

    A. Character

    B. Communion

    C. Community

    D. Conversation

40. Out of the eight recommended blog ideas - what would you start a blog about and why? (pg.48)

41. What is market research? (pg.50)

<u>Selling eBooks</u>

The internet has changed so many things in our world. Instead of fighting for parking or dealing with large crowds at shopping malls, we shop at Amazon.

Because of the internet, we can now use email to sell products and services. We can use Skype and Zoom to hold meetings and make a living from the comfort of our bed.

With the major advancements in every field and area, the book publishing industry has not been left behind. People can now start making money online through publishing and selling eBooks online. With Amazon Kindle, eBooks have become a booming business, and writers of all types are creating a name for themselves while making a nice income.

eBooks are books in a format that can be delivered or downloaded online. You can create eBooks from a variety of sources: write your own, hire authors, or compile public domain content. Your eBook can cover any topic under the sun, tailored to the theme of a niche market you have identified.

Anything you're passionate about and/or naturally gifted at can be packaged up as a guidebook, how-to, mystery, romance, science fiction, self-help, technology tipsheet or anything you can find an audience for.

As long as there is a market for aspiring buyers, almost every subject is a fair game. You can confirm this by scanning Amazon's bestseller list, which is broken down into hundreds of genre categories and subcategories.

One of the easiest ways to sell your eBook is to work through a third-party site like Amazon. It's free to publish a book on Amazon through their online Kindle Direct Publishing platform, making it a good start to making money online from a one-time creation!

This is the power of an eBook. **You create the content one time and have the ability to sell it over and over again.** You pay no upfront costs, but Amazon will take a portion of your book's earnings, leaving you with 35% to 70% of royalties depending on the retail price of your book. For example, if the price is $16, you'll earn $5.60 (35%), but if your book costs $9.99, you'll earn $6.99 (70%) for each sale.

From humble beginnings, eBooks now sell in the millions each year, with a global market worth more than $18 billion as of 2020. And there is plenty of room for a one-person eBook entrepreneur to get a piece of that pie!

You can also resell eBooks by other authors. Reselling an eBook is similar to the resale process of a physical text. Once you buy the eBook from a publisher or author, you have the right under normal resale rules to make the book available to your customers for purchase.

To increase eBook sales, focus on marketing strategies that are proven to attract customers. For example, you can distribute the first copy of a book for free. This helps to get the buzz on social media, get reviews, and attract customers through social proof.

Other effective strategies for promoting eBooks include influencer marketing and video campaigns via social media platforms.

<u>Transcription and Translation Services</u>

Transcribing and translating audio, video, and/or written word is a great way to bring in some extra cash on the side. Recall what I mentioned in the beginning. When conducting any type of business, the number-one purpose is to solve your customers' problems. The content creator has a problem, and you as the transcriber or translator has the solution!

First, let's clarify the difference between the two. **Transcription** is verbatim replication of spoken text in the same language. **Translation** means to re-create content into another language, carrying its meaning into the requested language.

You can make good money transcribing, and it's always in high demand, because this can be a very tedious and time-consuming task for the content creator.

If you're willing to put in the work to get good at it, then transcribing could provide you with an awesome work-at-home career that allows you to work anywhere in the world, whenever you want.

The translation market is an area waiting to be served. Translation comes in many forms, including word-for-word, verbatim, or literal. There is a lot less competition in this area than in other niche markets, mainly due to the barrier to entry. In order to take advantage of this opportunity, **you must be fluent in at least two languages.**

If you are bilingual or studying a popular language at school, this may be a great money-making idea to try. If you have a language degree or experience translating texts, be sure to emphasize this in your portfolio or resume. Most companies require translation tests and will not allow the use of translation tools to pass the tests.

Sites where you can find translation jobs to make money online include:

- Upwork
- People Per Hour
- Gengo
- Pro Translating
- Translators Base

Here are some tips for starting an online transcription or translation business.

Specialize your services. The most important step in starting any business is refining your idea so you know and understand your target audience. For example, I have started editing and helping people create podcasts. Unlike my finance teachings, which are for everyone, I was able to refine who I was talking to within my audience because the marketing I'm doing is only for people with a podcast.

Create a plan and a budget. If you fail to plan, then plan to fail! After niching down or refining who you will be helping, then you must create an actual plan to help them. What software will you need? Is a computer required? How will you communicate and take payment? All of those things should be answered before getting started.

Advertise and market. A common theme of all of the side hustles mentioned has been marketing! If no one knows who you are and what you do, then your business will never gain any traction. Start by posting and advertising on all social media platforms. From there, you can run paid ads and even market on freelance sites like Fivver and Upwork.

Build out a website. Your website doesn't have to be anything too crazy. A simple landing page where customers can learn your process, see your prices, and view your previous work can establish immense credibility.

<u>Creating Online Courses</u>

Selling courses is one of the best ways to make money online—and you don't need to be an expert! I always say, *anyone* can be an expert to someone who doesn't know what you know. For example, if you use techniques and strategies to raise your credit score to 700, then you can help anyone who has a credit score below 700!

If you're just a little more knowledgeable than the average person, or an actual expert, you can monetize your knowledge by creating online courses.

One great benefit of creating an online course, or anything digital, is that you can put in the work upfront and sell your product again and again. With physical items, you may need to create tons of products or purchase a boatload of inventory to sell. With digital products, you can create it one time and have the opportunity to make money for a lifetime!

Courses can be sold on the platforms Udemy, Gumroad, and Thinkific. If you already have an audience, you can sell it on your website or social media.

Take inspiration from courses offered in your niche to create popular and successful courses of your own. Look around on social media to see what other influencers are doing.

Pro tip: Purchase a very successful existing course to see what they're doing well and what can be improved on. From there, you can add your own spin and flavor to it.

Also, take a look at podcast reviews. What do people admire and dislike? Focus on creating content that resolves the most common complaints while emulating the positive aspects that people have praised.

The platform you choose to sell your course determines the best way to make money. If you sell a course on Udemy, you don't have to do much to promote it because of the large marketplace of potential buyers.

Advertising on blogs, YouTube, and social networks is always a good option. However, if your course is hosted on your website, it is best that you place an ad to promote your course to drive traffic to your offering.

Pro tip: Create an email mailing list to promote your course. Many entrepreneurs and influencers give out a free tool that incentivizes people to leave their email. Having your customers' email will make it much easier to communicate and advertise your course.

<u>Online Tutoring</u>

If you want to make money online on your own schedule, consider becoming an online tutor. According to a case study from Studenomics. com, a college student earned $2,100 in a semester by building a customer base through word-of-mouth, visibility, and excellent group rates for other students.

If you have a degree in education, you may be more likely to get a job as a tutor. If you don't have a degree or certification in this field, you'll need social proof of your abilities and expertise. **Social proof** comes through reviews and testimonials from previous customers about how well you can get the job done and the value that you provide.

While science and math are in high demand as tutoring subjects, you'll also find English is very popular among international audiences.

If you're an expert on a topic, tutoring may be the right platform for you to make money fast. **Thinkific** and **Teachable** are among the best platforms for online teaching.

Thinkific is a highly rated platform used to create, market, and sell your own online courses or membership sites. The platform has revolutionized how individuals earn and learn online by building an all-in-one platform designed for both course creators and their audiences. You can run live online classes, create courses, run an online membership site, and market courses all from one platform. Based on reviews, Thinkific wins for overall course website capabilities, managing bulk sales and content, and quiz/testing capabilities. Teachable wins for student engagement and interactivity, ease of navigation, selling/conversion tools, and customer support.

Data Entry Jobs: "Click Worker"

Data entry is one of the greatest ways to make extra cash from home in your spare time. It involves entering data into a computer system with a keyboard or smartphone. In addition, workers manage and maintain effective record keeping, organizing files to collect information for future use.

To start earning, enroll though on a popular freelancing site like **Fiverr.com** or **Upwork.com** listing the languages you are proficient in.

The equipment is pretty basic. Most important is a high-speed computer with high-speed Internet access. You may also want to use a good headset and a number pad for entering large volumes of numbers.

You won't need any fancy apps to be able to do these jobs, but you will need reliable applications software like Microsoft Office Suite. It's also a good idea to have some type of cloud storage facility to ensure your work is always backed up in case something goes missing. Dropbox and Google Drive are among the best cloud storage platforms out there that offer free space, but you can find many other no-cost alternatives.

One thing we haven't touched on: Regardless of the tools you choose, it's very important that your work environment is comfortable and suitable for carrying out your daily tasks. **This is critical for all remote opportunities that we have listed.**

As a workforce, none of us has ever been expected to sit still in our homes throughout most of the day as we do now. So it's imperative to have a designated workspace with a desk and chair that is designed for long periods of work. This will set clear boundaries, not only for your fellow household occupants, but for yourself as well.

Whenever you are at your desk, then your body knows it's time to work.

If you are working from the bed, then your body doesn't know when it is chill time or when it's work and productivity time. Whatever potential job you choose, create a special place where you can be productive and attentive. Set yourself up to do the best work possible without any added stressors.

Workbook: Chapter 3. Making Money Online

42. What is an eBook? (pg.53)

43. Transcribing and/or translating could provide you with an awesome work-at-home career that allows you to work anywhere in the world. — True or False (pg.55)

44. To make the most money from translating online you should be fluent in at least how many languages? (pg.55)

45. What problem could you solve by creating a course to help people in your neighborhood, city, state, or even the world? (pg.57)

46. What is social proof? (pg.58)

DIVIDEND INVESTING

Dividend investing is a method of buying stocks that pay dividends to receive a regular income stream from your investments. This income comes on top of any growth in your portfolio.

Dividends are payments made by a company to shareholders. They are powerful because you are literally being paid just to have part ownership in a company. How can you beat that?

Not all stocks give dividends to shareholders. If you own a stock that pays dividends, you get a portion of the company's profits. In addition to the growth of the market value, you can receive the flow of income. Suppose you want to invest in a company that pays a dividend of 3% per share. You buy a stake in the company worth $100. In this case, you will receive a dividend of $3.

Dividend investing can be a great investment strategy. Dividend stocks have historically outperformed the S&P 500 with less volatility. That's because dividend stocks provide two sources of return: **regular income from dividend payments** and **capital appreciation of the stock price.** This total return can add up over time.

To collect dividends on a stock, you simply need to own shares in the company through a brokerage account or a retirement plan such as an Individual Retirement Account (IRA) like a Roth or 401k. When the dividends are paid, the cash is automatically deposited into your account or reinvested back into the stock. This is called a DRIP—Dividend Reinvestment Plan.

How to Start Dividend Investing

Searching for "dividend yielding stocks" or "dividend aristocrats" online will generate a large list of stocks that offer dividend yields. To be considered an **"dividend aristocrat,"** businesses need to have a market capitalization of at least $3 billion and have increased dividends every year for the past 25 years. A **"dividend king"** is a company that has increased their dividends for the past 50 years!

Another option is dividend Exchange Trading Funds (ETFs). These are index funds that give investors exposure to various dividend stocks (basically a group of dividend stocks). These funds continue to pay dividends for all the stocks in the fund, providing built-in diversification.

Here are the four steps an investor can take to start dividend investing.

Step 1: Open a brokerage account. These days, opening a brokerage account online is easy and takes just a few minutes. Brokerage accounts are ideal for savings or goals that are further than five years away but closer than retirement, experts say. They can also complement an investor's emergency savings, according to the investment research firm Hearts & Wallets.

Some of the most prominent brokerages are Charles Schwab, Fidelity, E*TRADE, and M1 Finance.

Step 2: Fund the brokerage account. A brokerage account is an investment account that allows you to buy and sell a variety of investments such as stocks, bonds, mutual funds, and ETFs. To fund your account, you'll need to transfer money from a linked bank account such as your checking or savings. You may also be able to wire transfer money, deposit a check, or transfer investments from another broker.

Step 3: Buy a dividend stock. There are two main ways to invest in dividend stocks: Buying a group of stocks like mutual funds, index funds, or ETFs that hold dividend stocks or purchasing individual dividend stocks.

Step 4: Collect the dividends. The idea of collecting checks for the rest of your life and generating passive income can be very compelling. If this sounds like the type of investing strategy that appeals to you, you may want to look into investing as early as possible to build up the dividend income. Some people have built up dividend portfolios so big that their passive income is paying for their bills, vacations, and other expenses.

Top Tips for Investing in Dividend Stocks

Find sustainable dividends. Finding a sustainable dividend stock is one of the surest ways to avoid loss. Dividend aristocrats and dividend kings are less risky than newer companies offering dividends.

Reinvest those dividends. If you want to grow fast, don't accept the dividend payment. Put it back into the company to increase the amount of shares you own. This will make you an even bigger owner in the company, therefore increasing your dividend payout.

Don't fall for the "dividend trap." Do not be fooled by companies offering the highest dividend. Oftentimes this is called a **dividend trap**. Companies that are in trouble financially will offer an unusually high dividend to entice people to invest right before something catastrophic happens to that company. Instead, look for continued growth over the years and research their plans for the future. Don't stop there either. Check out the company's competition. If a certain company's dividend is much higher than a company in the same market, that usually means something is up.

Dividends help you generate income because they can be reinvested. They can also be used to pay for household necessities, pay for college, start a business, pay for vacations, and donate to charity.

Making Money from Dividend Stocks

Earning big on your dividend stocks involves a few key factors: **the dividend yield a stock offers at the time you buy it, the rate of growth in the company's profit, and the health of the company's financial balance sheet.**

The more profitable dividend stocks you own, the more money you can make. Income investors accumulate this particular type of investment over time. If you invest well, your net worth and income will continue to grow with the companies you've invested in.

Here are five simple tips to help you win big in dividend investments:

1. Live below your means. This step comes from the old saying, "It costs money to make money." Therefore, you must live under your means to generate extra money. This is a very simple formula: **Make more money, spend less, or both.** Living below your means creates extra cash flow. Go back to the Making Money Online section of this book for eight great ways to augment your income.

2. **Regularly invest and reinvest in dividend stocks.** Either select individual dividend stocks or choose to invest in one or more ETFs. Also, understand that going the ETF route will save time on investment research, increase diversification, and lessen risk. Although to clarify, I am not saying that identifying and selecting individual dividend stocks is a bad idea, just a more time-sensitive one.

Importantly, make sure you reinvest all dividends. Either automatically channel dividends back into the stock that paid them or let the dividends accumulate in cash until you are ready to deposit funds into the stock of your choice. Just don't take the dividends that are paid and spend them.

3. **Keep investment costs low.** First, regardless of whether you choose individual dividend stocks or funds, **never pay a per-share commission to trade your stocks.** Commissions are simply not necessary—not even for do-it-yourself dividend investors like you and me. It's easy to sign up and fund your account. After you do, buy your stocks for free. Second, if you decide to get your dividend payments through funds like ETFs or index funds, make sure to choose funds with **low expense ratios.**

4. **Defer income taxes.** One of the fastest ways to get rich with dividends is to take advantage of every tax break available. That means, for example, buying and holding your dividend stocks in a traditional IRA.

Everyone's situation is a little different, when it comes to taxes. So, it's best to consult with a tax advisor. Nevertheless, here are a couple of thoughts to consider that apply to everyone: A traditional IRA account allows the investor to contribute on a pre-tax basis from earned income, just like a 401k, where invested income from your job avoids taxation. So, you have more left over to invest.

Second, consider buying investments through a Roth IRA. This allows your money to grow tax free and you won**'t have to pay** taxes when pulling your money out during retirement age.

5. **Practice patience.** Dividend investing is a journey, not a destination. As mentioned, time is the biggest factor when it comes to any type of investing. It will take years, patience, and discipline to get rich with dividend investing. This is not a get-rich-quick scheme, although you

can get rich slowly. If you really want to win with dividends, buckle up and get ready for a long, but worthy road trip.

<u>Protecting Your Investments</u>

Your goal with dividend investments is to generate positive returns while protecting yourself from major losses. So how do you really protect your investment?

Diversify your investments. As you learn more about the different investment options, you may develop some favorites. Some stocks may sound more exciting than others, but avoid investing all your money in one place. I'm sure you've heard the term, "Never put all your eggs into one basket." Same thing here! Diversification is the key to protecting yourself from big losses.

For example, if you make a high-risk investment in some new technology start-ups, you should also make a low-risk investment to offset potential losses. Bonds, CDs, pensions, and investment trusts are good examples.

Evaluate your risk tolerance. Investment diversification is ideal for many investors. However, if you have a low-risk appetite, you should consider investing mostly in low-risk investment products. A long-term safe investment can bring both security and sound benefits.

Both U.S. savings and municipal bonds are government-backed and low-risk options. CDs and investment trusts are other products to consider. Understand that low-risk investments have lower returns, but slow and steady investments can be a valuable strategy for some investors.

Choose long-term investing over short-term. By diversifying your investments over time, you have more opportunities for growth. Investing for 10 years compared to 1 year can make a difference between $7,000 and $200,000 in earnings.

As the value of your investments increase, so does your money. Consider how compound interest affects HYSAs. When interest is accumulated in your balance, you can earn even more as it recycles and builds up.

Establish a trust fund. Setting up a trust fund is a great way to protect your investments. To get started, you will select a trustee to manage the trust on your behalf. A trustee can be an individual, an institution (bank or trust company), or a combination of the two.

Trust funds can hold most assets, including cash, investment accounts, stock, and real estate. You decide how you want your assets distributed, with as many restrictions as you wish. This ensures that when the time comes, all your assets are transferred to the right people. A trust can also help reduce tax obligations and probate expenses, leaving more of your money intact.

Workbook: Chapter 3. (Dividend Investing)

47. What is a dividend? (pg.61)

48. All companies pay dividends for owning a share of their company? True or False (pg.61)

49. What two forms of income can you receive from owning a dividend stock? (pg.61)

50. What is the first step to investing in a dividend stock? (pg.62)

51. The two main ways to invest in dividend stocks are: (pg.62)

52. Some people have built up dividend portfolios so big that their passive income is paying their bills, vacations, and other expenses. True or False (pg.63)

53. What is a "dividend trap": (pg.62)

54. Making money from dividend stocks involves a handful of key factors like: (pg.63)

CHAPTER 4: HOW TO MANAGE MONEY DURING AN ECONOMIC DOWNFALL

Budgeting is one of the most important financial habits you can adopt. If you've never lived on a budget, or experienced all the benefits that budgeting has to offer, it's easy to wonder why it's such a prominent aspect of personal finance.

Simply, a budget is **a spending plan based on your income and expenses.** In other words, it's an estimate of how much money you'll make and spend over a certain period of time, such as a month or year.

Creating this spending plan allows you to determine in advance whether you will have enough money to do the things you need to do or would like to do. **Most people view a budget as a life restrictor, but I believe budgeting is a life enabler!** Once you have your budget in place, it is much easier to understand what is going into your account (Income) and what is going out (Expenses).

A budget is a strategic plan for achieving a particular goal by making the best use of the resources you have available. Whether you have a lot of money or a little, budgeting builds financial stability through control and maintenance of financial resources. **Without a budget, it will be incredibly difficult to control your spending, track your expenses, and save more money.**

Most people agree that the world revolves around money, and if it doesn't in your opinion, think about this: You need a roof over your head, transportation, and food to eat, which all cost money. With that being said, we should be striving to control our money so it doesn't control us!

Here's a list of the most important reasons to create a budget (for those who are list-lovers like myself):

1. It helps you keep your eye on the prize.

2. It helps ensure you don't spend money you don't have.

3. It puts you in control of your money.

4. It helps prioritize your life choices.

5. It ensures you get control of debt or avoid future bad debt.

6. It helps you be prepared for unexpected emergencies.

7. It helps lead to a happier retirement.

8. It helps shed light on bad spending habits.

HOW TO MAKE A BUDGET

There are **three** main budget categories of spending.

Needs. These are expenses that you must pay in order to live and work, such as a mortgage, rent, and car maintenance. This category should account for 50% of your spending.

Wants. These are expenses that don't qualify as needs and don't include your savings and payments toward debt. If you can live and make money without it, it's probably a want. This category should account for 30% of your spending.

Wants vary from person to person and from situation to situation, and so sometimes it can be hard to distinguish them from needs. For example, if you use a bike to get to work every day, the price of upkeep is a need. If you use a bike for fun and leisure only, it's a want.

Savings and debt repayment. The two biggest deterrents to building wealth are taxes and debt. As for debt, focus first on any toxic debt you may have, such as high-interest credit cards, personal and payday loans, car title loans, and rent-to-own payments.

Although paying down debt is critical to building wealth, so is investing and saving. We should not prolong or skip out on any of the three on this financial journey we are on.

Our dollar will never be as powerful as it is today. It has been proven that time is the biggest factor when it comes to building wealth, so the earlier we start saving, investing, and getting rid of debt the better.

A basic rule of thumb for budgeting is to divide your monthly after-tax income into these three spending categories: 50% for **needs**, 30% for **wants** and 20% for **savings or paying off debt.** This is called the **50-30-20 rule**. While these are great starting points, this method can be customized to fit your personal situation. I mean hey, they call it PERSONAL finance for a reason!

I believe that the 50-30-20 rule is great for anyone who has trouble starting a budget. But for those who have trouble sticking to one, I recommend the **lifestyle budget.**

In my opinion, a lifestyle budget is the simplest way to budget, and it's the method I personally use to this day.

To build a lifestyle budget, you first need to understand what is going in and what is going out—**income vs. expenses**. Your income will be all the money you are making from a job, business, or side hustle. Your expenses are everything you spend your money on. By going back through your last three months of bank statements, you can track and record what you truly spend your money on.

Once you have accounted for how you spend your money, the next step is to create two categories: **mandatory expenses** and **spendable income.** Then add up what you normally spend each month based on the average of the previous three months, including a $200–$500 cushion designated for miscellaneous expenses.

This is a good buffer to have, because while it's very easy to account for our fixed expenses like a car note, cell phone bill, and rent, it is very difficult to plan for the variable expenses that change every month like eating out, shopping, vet bills, and other spontaneous events that can't always be anticipated. This is where budgeting for the unknown can make your life easier and less stressful.

So, after you combine your normal expenses with your miscellaneous expenses,and have included your saving and investing then you get your spendable income amount. After you account for your mandatory expenses, whatever's left over is money that can be spent on anything you want!

Whether you have $200 or $2,000 left over, that money can be spent guilt-free because you know and understand that you have everything necessary covered through your mandatory expenses category.

<u>How to Budget Using Paper or Excel</u>

It's easy to use an electronic or paper spreadsheet to track your spending and stay on track.

1. List the budget items and their dollar amounts.

2. Record the amount that was actually spent for each budget item.

3. Write a description for each budget item that you spent money on.

4. Summarize the money you planned to spend compared to what you actually spent

5. If you have money left over - great job!

6. If you are in the negative - no worries! We either need to cut back on spending or find a way to make more money.

Example of a simple budget.

Monthly cost:

____

Rent

$1,000

Home expenses

$100

Home repairs

$50

Car Insurance

$25

____

Income $2,000

Expenses: $1,175

Spendable Income: $825

Ways to Stick to a Budget

One reason many budgets fail is because the user finds it difficult to stick to it. Don't worry, every human on this planet falls short of perfection, so don't beat yourself up.

Budgeting requires you to set limits on your spending, so when you have income that varies on a monthly basis, it can be especially hard to stay on target.

Of course, there are tons of tips and tricks to sticking to your budget every month. But following "tons" is hard. Below are the best eight ways to keep you on track.

Calculate your net income. The foundation of an effective budget is your net income. Net income is what you have after all your taxes and pre-tax deductions. This number can give you a more realistic idea of how much you can afford to spend, save, and pay in taxes.

Set up auto draft payments. Set up automatic payments from your bank account and pay as many monthly bills as you can as soon as you get your paycheck. This is such a good idea because it begins a small habit that can yield large results for you in the future.

Set up automatic payments for saving and investing. Let technology do the work for you, so you don't have to spend time and energy on remembering to do them manually! This is the most painless way to save your income: silently, regularly, and automatically.

Keep it real. Have you ever made a goal that totally set you up for failure? Like promising to run 10 miles a day all year when you haven't run 1 mile since middle school? If you want to succeed, you have to push yourself, but you also have to be realistic. The same is true with your budget. Push yourself to spend better and save more but be realistic when you set up your spending plan.

For example, if you normally spend $400 eating out, let's try to decrease that by $50, then $100, and keep making your way down as it gets easier. Making small, incremental adjustments that you can stay consistent with will pay off much more than jumping to huge goals. When you keep it real, you can really win.

Make a plan for spending your money. Planning well in advance how to use your money helps you navigate tricky situations, avoid impulsive spending, meet financial obligations, and build wealth. It is vital because stable budgeting provides financial security and freedom and secures you in a financial emergency.

Adjust your spending to stay on budget. Ideally, you should reflect on whether your budget is working for you whenever you get paid. A budget is an ongoing process, so you should definitely be auditing your previous budget that you made and use that to make your next one.

Learn to say no (or not now). Don't worry about what everyone on social media is doing. A lot of these influencers are lying. Many are in debt and very few really do have their lives together. But those people worked hard for the money and that's what you're going to do too—but manage it better!

Work hard defending your budget by saying no or not now when you need to. Being true to yourself, your budget, and your money goals is more valuable than flexing for people you don't know and that you may not even like.

Review your budget regularly. Reviewing and adjusting your budget helps you to better manage your spending habits, increase your savings, and make progress toward your long-term financial goals. It's an important component of proper money management and a key element of personal finance. What it means to review your budget is comparing actual vs. planned spending, assessing new income and expenses, and planning for unexpected events that may be on the horizon.

Workbook: Chapter 4. Budgeting

55. What is a budget: (pg.68)

56. Name three benefits of budgeting: (pg.68)

57. What are the three main budget categories to include in your budget? (pg.69)

58. What is net income? (pg.69)

59. On pg.72-73, out of the eight ways to stick to a budget which do you feel is the most important?

MANAGING MONEY BY SAVING

"It's not about how much money we can make, it's about how much money we can save!"

Saving is the portion of income not spent on current expenditures. In other words, it's the money set aside for future use and not to be spent immediately. Saving money is important because it helps cushion the blow of financial emergencies and unexpected expenses.

Growing up, my dad instructed me to save at least 50% of my income. Me, being a young high school student, did not listen. Looking back on it now, I believe the reason I didn't take his advice was because I truly didn't understand why I should save money—and what happens if I don't!

Speaking to someone about money, health, or personal fitness can be taboo, even today. We know we should be working out, and we know we should be saving money. But what I have found when talking about these topics is that we have to discuss both the pros of doing the positive action, and the cons of NOT doing the positive action. In my opinion, this is what will create true change and action.

The pros of saving money:

- **Peace of mind.** Knowing you have money to fall back on when, not if, something unexpected happens is what creates that feeling of true peace of mind.

- **Retirement.** Retirement may be years off or it could be right around the corner for some of you reading this, **but it is never too late or too early to start saving for retirement.** Whether it's a business, athletic career, a music career, or a large sum of money, it takes time to build anything great! The earlier we start, the less stress and worry that we put on ourselves in the future, so show yourself some self-love by saving early and often!

- **Compounding interest.** Your money, making more money on the initial money saved or invested. That's all there is to compound interest, but the only way to truly take advantage of it is to save as early as possible. The longer our money sits in an asset that appreciates or rises in value, the better.

The cons of NOT saving money:

- **Dependency:** What happens when your tire blows out? What happens when you get really sick and can't work? Who are you going to rely on? With no money saved for emergencies, you put yourself in a position to lose. You may have to borrow from a bank, a parent, spouse, or significant other. If you've ever borrowed money from someone, then you know there are always some extra stipulations to that money you're borrowing. To alleviate this problem, create an emergency fund for those "just in case" moments so there is no added stress or anxiety to an already unfortunate situation.

- **Broke in retirement:** Who wants to grow old with no money? Enough said. Actually, I have one thing to add to that. For my younger readers, there is something called Social Security. Social Security is a fixed amount of money given monthly to people who are retired from the workforce. Unfortunately for Millennials and Gen Z, many projections state that the Social Security treasury will be empty by the time we retire. With that being said, we must look out for ourselves now and in the future by saving and investing.

Poor quality of life: Living paycheck to paycheck, borrowing from high-interest lenders, and having no time or option to do as you please are all consequences of failing to save. We are put on this earth to live an abundant lifestyle, and to do that we must have money to spend, but also money to be put up and saved for emergencies.

Additionally, saving money can help you pay for large purchases, avoid debt, reduce your financial stress, and provide you with a greater sense of financial freedom.

<u>Six Easy Ways to Save Money</u>

1. Preplanning

Preplanning is deciding how to get something done before starting on it. An example of preplanning is making a list of how you're going to accomplish everything you want to do in your day. Preplanning provides you with the time needed to make practical, detailed decisions that reflect your lifestyle, taste, and budget.

Having a plan gives you the confidence and competency that you're going into whatever situation prepared and ready to execute. Having no plan and just going with the flow can cause stress, nervousness, and even full-blown anxiety.

Planning ahead is really the best way to save money. The choices you make based on a well-thought-out plan will be carried out more efficiently than those made without one. Paying for vacations, sporting events, and even medical visits are all easier when we've planned the expense ahead of time.

We know these events are going to happen far in advance, so instead of waiting until right before an event to decide how to pay for it, why not start early by putting a small amount to the side?

When you finalize your plan, you will understand the total cost. But if we wait until the event is near, we put ourselves in a bind, pulling money that should be going to rent, bills, food, etc. This usually leaves us with very little money after the trip or special event, and I don't want that for you.

Here are some tips on planning ahead that will save money in a variety of situations:

- Plan your grocery shopping with a list

- Plan your meals (meal prep)

- Shop with a plan

- Eat out with a purpose

Basically, plan your spending. This will prevent you from buying what you don't need and suffering remorse.

Allow me to elaborate on this a bit more.

First, let's acknowledge there are some things in our personal lives that we truly love and enjoy. If you really love Starbucks, that's fine, just be aware of that spending habit. Include your daily Starbucks run in your budget and plan for it. If it fits in your budget, and you're not spending more money than you make then you're doing fine! **A daily Starbucks coffee will not stop you from becoming financially free, unless you don't PLAN for it!**

Planning ahead is critical when you're striving to live better on less. Planning is important, it sounds cliche but if you fail to plan, you can't check out how you are doing.

In short, when you fail to plan, you plan to fail. Therefore, if you are someone who really wants to save and work towards a worry-free life, preplanning is a skill you should definitely buckle down on.

2. Use a separate high-yield savings account

Depositing money in a savings account has very little risk. As you've heard before, with high risk comes high reward. Well, in this scenario it's the exact opposite, but stay with me. Putting money in your regular-degular savings account at your traditional bank is just not the move anymore. **Most banks are providing us with interest rates of 0.003%.** This is literally close to nothing. As we know from 6th grade math, zero times zero will always be ZERO!

So where should you be saving, if it's not with your bank that you've probably had for years? The answer to that is in an **HYSA**. This is literally the same type of account as you have at your bank, but it gives you more bang for your buck! You can get an interest rate of 2% to 3% while your money is securely saved.

High yield saving accounts (HYSAs) are usually associated with online banks, which can afford these rates because they avoid the costs of a bricks-and-mortar location. This saves them tons of time and money, which they fortunately pass on to us in the form of higher savings rates than traditional banks.

Another benefit of keeping your checking and savings accounts separate is to avoid the temptation of dipping into your savings for non-emergency items. It's a way to protect yourself from yourself.

Three advantages of using a savings account are 1) the potential to earn interest, 2) easy to open and access, and 3) FDIC insured savings. Requiring a minimum balance is another advantage of opening a savings account, since there is no way you can empty your account, making it the best way of saving money.

3. Use a "spare change" program

Another great way to save is to automate your savings so you don't even have to think about it! We have plenty of things that take our time and energy, so let's find ways to set it and forget it!

One of the best ways to build up your savings is to make additions to it on a regular basis. The Acorns app is a fintech platform that allows customers to save money automatically in a simple, hands-off way. Every time you use your debit card connected to the app, the purchase total is rounded up, and that extra money is saved. So, when you spend $4.76 on a morning coffee, 24 cents will be sent to an automated investment account that you own.

This feature is so cool, because every time you spend—you save! Now you may be thinking, 24 cents—that's nothing, but Acorns or any type of saving that is done automatically truly does add up! If you save 25 cents, five times a day, you can save hundreds over a year.

While in college, I actually forgot I had the Acorns app for a while. An emergency came up, and I was looking for money. I did not want to borrow or ask my family for anything, so I checked my Acorns app and I had $500 dollars saved up—which only took about seven months!

This is why having an emergency fund or peace of mind fund is so critical. After realizing I had this money to fall back on, tons of stress and anxiety literally evaporated. Make a one-time decision that will impact you positively for the rest of your life by automating your savings!

4.   Invest in the stock market

Investing in the stock market is another place for money to grow. In exchange for your money, companies issue shares. Owning a share means you now hold or own a portion of the company.

Stock-market based investments tend to do better than cash over the long term, providing an opportunity for greater returns on any money invested over time. **The stock market has a proven track record, producing a 7% to 10% return on money invested. over the last 100 years.**

Remember earlier when we talked about saving in a traditional bank? Those banks give .003%, while the stock market on average has returned at least 7% over this last century. However, remember that's just an average across the entire market—some years will be up, some will be down, and individual stocks will vary in their returns.

Year-over-year returns should not be an issue or stressor for us long-term investors. We know throughout the years, long-term investing has been proven to win out over a period of time.

Disclaimer: This is not investment advice. I repeat...**not investment advice.**

I want to tell you about my favorite type of stock market investment. It is called an ETF which is an abbreviation for exchange-traded funds. I've mentioned them before. Simply, **an ETF is investing in a group of stocks** compared to investing in an individual stock.

The example that I love to use is this: Imagine investing in an individual stock like Tesla. Tesla has a very successful, yet controversial CEO named

Elon Musk. If Elon happened to do something that many people didn't like, that would not only make the stock price of Tesla drop, but the value of your investment in Tesla would drop as well!

I use this example because if you were to invest in an ETF that holds shares of Nike, Walmart, Coke, *and* Tesla, your money would not be impacted significantly by Elon's questionable decisions because of those other strong companies that you're invested in.

That is my favorite way to show the huge benefit of investing in an ETF (group of stocks) compared to an individual stock. The other major benefits are lower risk and cost, tax benefits, and diversification as we mentioned.

Here is a list of some top ETFs to check out:

- iShares ETFs

- SPDR ETFs

- Vanguard ETFs

- Invesco ETFs

- Blackrock ETFs

5. Buy real estate

Real estate is one of the greatest sources of wealth and savings. **Ninety percent** of millionaires made their wealth and preserved their wealth this way.

Real estate investors make money through rental income, value appreciation, and profits generated by business activities that depend on the property.

The benefits of investing in real estate include passive income, stable cash flow, tax advantages, diversification, and leverage. Because of the many tax benefits, real estate investing often ends up costing less in taxes overall even as it brings considerable income.

One of my favorite sayings is: The **two biggest deterrents to building wealth are taxes and debt.**

Maybe this is why real estate is so beneficial. You acquire debt and then use that debt to make money that comes in forever, while using real estate tax strategies to lower the amount of taxes you have to give to Uncle Sam. Not only does real estate make you money, but it allows you to keep a lot more of the money you make!

Property is a great place to park your money because it's likely to increase in value consistently over time and mostly outperforms other investments. Most millionaires make more money from owning real estate than other investments. Besides saving money, you may even use it as a part of your overall strategy to begin building wealth. In my view, it's wise to consider buying real estate when looking for ways to make your money work for you.

6. Buying Treasury inflation-protected securities

A Treasury inflation-protected security (TIPS) is a Treasury bond that mimics an inflationary gauge to protect investors from the decline in the purchasing power of their money—a.k.a. inflation. The principal value of TIPS rises as inflation rises while the interest payment varies with the adjusted principal value of the bond. When a TIPS matures, you are paid the adjusted principal or original principal, whichever is greater.

TIPS can be a good investment choice when inflation is running high, since they adjust payments when interest rates rise, whereas other bonds don't. This is usually a good strategy for short-term investing, but stocks and other investments may offer better long-term returns.

If you want to buy TIPS, you can get them through your online brokerage account or directly from the U.S. Treasury at www.treasurydirect.gov/. If you choose to buy TIPS on the secondary market, be sure to compare how much the current inflation-adjusted par value—the face value of a bond—differs from the original par value. The fact that TIPS are never affected by inflation means that it is a good way to invest and save money during an up or down market.

Workbook: Chapter 4. Saving

60. Why is saving money important? (pg.75)

61. Pg.76 talks about the impact of NOT saving. Which reason is the most convincing for you?

62. Think of a time when you pre planned for something compared to when you didn't prepare...What were the outcomes? Which worked better? (pg.77)

63. Pre-planning provides you with the time needed to make practical and detailed decisions that reflect your standards, lifestyle, taste, and budget which will lead to less stress and healthier outcomes. True or False (pg.77)

64. What are the three advantages of using a savings accounts: (pg.78)

65. Over the last decade, the stock market has averaged what percentage of return on money invested? (pg.79)

66. What are the benefits of investing into real estate? (pg.80)

67. Why is a Treasury Inflation-Protected Security (TIPS) a good choice compared to an ordinary bond (pg.81)

FINAL THOUGHTS

To wrap everything up for my FYI FLI folks, life has taught, brought, and taken many things to and from us, but we have a choice. We can take what is handed to us and accept it without question, or we can accept what life gives us and use that to go TAKE what we truly deserve.

I am so happy and proud that you are taking your time to learn and educate yourself on financial literacy, investing, and entrepreneurship. I want you to continue to grow and explore alternative learning methods, but soaking up information is not the end-all, be-all. We actually have to put that information into action because **education without implementation is worthless!**

There is no experience greater than hands-on experience. So, after reading this book—**go get active**!

One of our most-used sayings on our podcast is to "Make a plan and make a play." That's how simple life can be: Analyze the situation, plan your moves, then execute. But remain flexible, because unforeseen issues will occur!

COVID and the recession have taught us to expect the unexpected! It's a fact that we will experience another recession. We will experience another pandemic. I hope you will use the things you've learned and experiences you've gone through to make better decisions for you and your family.

No matter what, keep being a blessing and keep progressing!

Stay Safe.

Stay Invested.

Stay FYI FLI!

HASSAN R. THOMAS

EMAIL
INFO@HASSANRTHOMAS.COM

- bulk book sales
- media interviews
- podcast advertising
- speaking opportunities
- teaching opportunities

CONNECT ON SOCIAL MEDIA

Facebook/Instagram:
@ceosanni
@fyifli

LinkedIn:
@Hassan Thomas

Podcast:
https://kite.link/FYIFLI

Websites:
www.fyifli.com
www.hassanrthomas.com

YouTube:
FYI FLI

FYI
FLI
THE PODCAST
FYI S
Season 1-3
Available on all major
streaming platforms
SEA 2022 Podcast of the Year

From College to COVID To Recession
A Guide to Making & Managing Money During an Economic Downfall (KEY)

Chapter 1: From College to COVID

1. Hassan gave 5 major lessons going 'From College To Covid': **Keep faith in a higher power, provide value, eliminate distractions, live in reality, and embrace fear**

Which lesson can you relate to the most and why?

2. What has been your biggest lesson learned after going through COVID and quarantine?

3. Did you uncover any skills or passions? How can you turn that passion into profit?

Chapter 2: Recession

4. List some ways a recession could impact you? (pg.18)

   A: Continued inflation, which makes everything more expensive, and the potential to lose your job.

5. True or False: You should pull all your money out of investments during a recession and save only cash (pg.18)

   A: False

6. What is a simple way to define a recession? (pg.19)

A: A recession is defined by two consecutive negative quarters (6 months) of declining Gross Domestic Product (GDP).

7. What is Gross Domestic Product (GDP) (pg.19)

A: GDP is a calculation of all the goods, services, and products a country has produced quarterly or annually; or GDP is the total production of a country.

8. What are the four major expenditures that categorize GDP? (pg.19)

A: Consumer expenditure, business and investment expenditure, government expenditure, and net imports and exports.

9. What are the three factors that makeup recessions? (pg.19)

A: High unemployment, high inflation, and high interest rates.

10. What is the money called that you make from a job, side hustle, or business? (pg.21)

   A. *Profit*

   B. *Revenue*

   C. Income

   D. *Expense*

11. What is the money called that you spend? (pg.21)

   A. *Dividend*

   B. Expense

   C. *Income*

   D. *Gone*

12. What is the money called that's available to spend after mandatory expenses are paid? (pg.21)

13. Why is it good to have a plan? (pg.21)

14. True or False: The worst time to do emergency planning is in the middle of an emergency. (pg.22)

15. What is a "peace of mind" fund"? (pg.22)

   A: A set amount of money that you build for when, not if, something unexpected happens.

16. Where is the best place to keep your "Peace of Mind Fund"?(pg.22)

17. Why does job loss impact us during a recession? (pg.23)

18. The most effective way to combat job loss is by investing in: (pg.23)

   A. Stocks

   B. Real Estate

   C. Yourself

   D. Crypto

19. The more you LEARN - the more you EARN? True or False (pg.23)

20. What is inflation? (pg.25)

21. In this particular recession, why does the government want us to refrain from spending money at a fast rate? (pg.25)

22. What is macroeconomics? (pg.30)

23. What is microeconomics? (pg.30)

24. Why is it important to be knowledgeable about what's going on in the world? (pg.30)

25. What happens when The Federal Reserve "The Fed" increases interest rates? (pg.31)

26. What is the purpose of raising interest rates? (pg.31)

27. What happens if The Federal Reserve increases interest rates too much? (pg.31)

28. What does interest mean? (pg.32)

29. When interest rates rise they help people that are saving and investing - they also significantly cripple and punish people who are borrowing and in heavy debt! True or False (pg.32)

30. Which recession lasted the longest? (pg.34)

31. Which recession is known as the worst ever? (pg.35)

32. Which recession is closely associated with our current recession? (pg.35)

33. Due to the recession our everyday items like food, gas, and housing cost the same as the year before? True or False (pg.35)

34. What is fear-mongering? (pg.36)

35. According to the CEO of Centsai Financial Education, Arindam Nag, how much should we save? (pg.37)

36. Why should we save money? (pg.37)

Chapter 3. Making Money Online

37. Drop shipping is a good business model because you can avoid paying for shipping and store inventory. True or False (pg.43)

38. What are the three parties involved with drop shipping? (pg.43)

   A. **The customer, The drop shipper (you), and The third-party supplier.**

   B. The consumer, The director, and The fulfiller

   C. The creator, The distributor, and The fiddler

   D. The customer, The dump taker, and The third-party supplier.

39. One of the biggest keys to creating a blog is to establish a: (pg.47)

   A. Character

   B. Communion

   C. Community

   D. Conversation

40. Out of the eight recommended blog ideas - what would you start a blog about and why? (pg.48)

41. What is market research? (pg.50)

42. What is an eBook? (pg.53)

43. Transcribing and/or translating could provide you with an awesome work-at-home career that allows you to work anywhere in the world. — True or False (pg.55)

44. To make the most money from translating online you should be fluent in at least how many languages? (pg.55)

45. What problem could you solve by creating a course to help people in your neighborhood, city, state, or even the world? (pg.57)

46. What is social proof? (pg.58)

Chapter 3 (Dividend Investing):

47. What is a dividend? (pg.61)

48. All companies pay dividends for owning a share of their company? True or False (pg.61)

49. What two forms of income can you receive from owning a dividend stock? (pg.61)

50. What is the first step to investing in a dividend stock? (pg.62)

51. The two main ways to invest in dividend stocks are: (pg.62)

52. Some people have built up dividend portfolios so big that their passive income is paying their bills, vacations, and other expenses. True or False (pg.63)

53. What is a "dividend trap": (pg.63)

54. Making money from dividend stocks involves a handful of key factors like: (pg.63)

Chapter 4 Budgeting:

55. What is a budget: (pg.68)

56. Name three benefits of budgeting: (pg.68)

    A. It helps you keep your eye on the prize.

    B. It helps ensure you don't spend money you don't have..

    C. It puts you in control of your money.

    D. It helps prioritize your life

    E. It ensures you get control of debt or avoid future bad debt.

    F. It helps you be prepared for unexpected emergencies.

    G. It helps lead to a happier retirement.

    H. It helps shed light on bad spending habits

57. What are the three main budget categories to include in your budget? (pg.69)

58. 58. What is net income? (pg.69)

59. On pg.72-73, out of the eight ways to stick to a budget which do you feel is the most important?

Chapter 4 Saving:

60. Why is saving money important? (pg.75)

61. Pg.76 talks about the impact of NOT saving. Which reason is the most convincing for you?

62. Think of a time when you pre planned for something compared to when you didn't prepare...What were the outcomes? Which worked better? (pg.77)

63. Pre-planning provides you with the time needed to make practical and detailed decisions that reflect your standards, lifestyle, taste, and budget which will lead to less stress and healthier outcomes. True or False (pg.77)

64. What are the three advantages of using a savings accounts: (pg.78)

65. Over the last decade, the stock market has averaged what percentage of return on money invested? (pg.79)

66. What are the benefits of investing into real estate? (pg.80)

67. Why is a Treasury Inflation-Protected Security (TIPS) a good choice compared to an ordinary bond (pg.81)

www.ingramcontent.com/pod-product-compliance
Lightning Source LLC
Chambersburg PA
CBHW051128160726

47997CB00018B/829

* 9 7 9 8 9 8 5 5 1 2 3 9 7 *